High Protein Vegan

OVER **100** HEALTHY PLANT-BASED RECIPES

ROSE WYLES
THE VEGAN NUTRITIONIST

hamlyn

hamlyn

First published in Great Britain in 2024
by Hamlyn, an imprint of
Octopus Publishing Group Ltd
Carmelite House
50 Victoria Embankment
London EC4Y 0DZ
www.octopusbooks.co.uk

An Hachette UK Company
www.hachette.co.uk

This material was previously published
in *HAC: 200 200 Cakes and Bakes*,
HAC: 200 Cupcakes, *HAC: 200 Delicious
Desserts*, *HAC: 200 Easy Vegetarian
Dishes*, *HAC: 200 Fast Vegetarian
Recipes*, *HAC: 200 One Pot Meals*,
HAC: 200 Really Easy Recipes, *HAC:
200 Student Meals*, *HAC: 200 Vegan
Recipes* and *HAC: 200 Veggie Feasts*.

Copyright © Octopus Publishing
Group Ltd 2024

Distributed in the US by
Hachette Book Group
1290 Avenue of the Americas
4th and 5th Floors, New York, NY 10104

Distributed in Canada by
Canadian Manda Group, 664 Annette St.
Toronto, Ontario, Canada M6S 2C8

ISBN 978-0-600-63864-3

A CIP catalogue record for this book is
available from the British Library.

Printed and bound in China.

10 9 8 7 6 5 4 3 2 1

Commissioning Editor: Louisa Johnson
Editor: Scarlet Furness
Copy Editor: Jo Richardson
Editorial Assistant: Constance Lam
Art Directors: Nicky Collings and
    Jaz Bahra
Designer: Aaron Blecha
Deputy Picture Manager: Jennifer Veall
Assistant Production Manager:
    Allison Gonsalves

Standard level spoon measurements
are used in all recipes.
1 tablespoon = one 15 ml spoon
1 teaspoon = one 5 ml spoon

Both imperial and metric
measurements have been given in all
recipes. Use one set of measurements
only and not a mixture of both.

Fresh herbs should be used unless
otherwise stated. If unavailable use
dried herbs as an alternative but halve
the quantities stated.

Ovens should be preheated to the
specific temperature – if using a fan-
assisted oven, follow manufacturer's
instructions for adjusting the time and
the temperature.

Pepper should be freshly ground black
pepper unless otherwise stated.

This book includes dishes made with
nuts and nut derivatives. It is advisable
for those with known allergic reactions
to nuts and nut derivatives and those
who may be potentially vulnerable
to these allergies, such as pregnant
and nursing mothers, the elderly,
babies and children, to avoid dishes
made with nuts and nut oils. It is also
prudent to check the labels of pre-
prepared ingredients for the possible
inclusion of nut derivatives.

Contents

4 INTRODUCTION

Why follow a plant-based diet?

What are the benefits of plant-based proteins?

How much protein do you need?

Protein-packed plant-based ingredients

High-protein vegan ingredient swaps

Achieving a balanced high-protein vegan diet

10 WEEKLY MEAL PLANS

14 POWER BREAKFASTS

40 SNACKS & QUICK BITES

62 ENERGIZING LUNCHES

88 DELICIOUS DINNERS

114 TASTY SWEET TREATS

140 GLOSSARY OF UK/US TERMS

142 INDEX

144 ABOUT THE AUTHOR

144 BIBLIOGRAPHY

Introduction

This cookbook explores the amazing power of plant protein. Whether you are new to a plant-based lifestyle, a dedicated vegan or simply looking to supplement your diet with plant protein-packed dishes, here you will find a wide variety of delicious and nutritious recipes to help you attain and maintain your optimal daily protein intake. Adopting a vegan diet doesn't mean abandoning your favourite flavours or compromising your health. On the contrary – you will discover a whole new range of tasty meals for every day that benefit your health and well-being.

It has never been easier to incorporate high-protein foods into a vegan diet, and these specially designed recipes demonstrate how to achieve that while enjoying flavourful and satisfying meals. By following the carefully crafted meal plans on pages 10–13, you can be confident in knowing that your body is getting all the nutrients it needs to thrive on a vegan diet for a set number of calories suitable for your energy requirements. Welcome to the wonderful world of high-protein vegan meals!

WHY FOLLOW A PLANT-BASED DIET?

The vegan diet consists of fruits, vegetables, whole grains, legumes, herbs, spices and any other foods that exclude animal products like meat, dairy, eggs and honey. Veganism has become popular in recent years due to its scientifically proven health benefits, ethical considerations and focus on environmental sustainability. Most people are drawn to a veganism out of concern for animal rights, but many now commit to a vegan diet to reduce their environmental impact as well as improve their health.

When we choose a vegan diet, we are supporting sustainable agriculture and helping to mitigate the devastating environmental impact that animal agriculture has on our precious planet. By reducing our reliance on animal proteins, we can decrease our carbon footprint associated with food production and contribute to an economically viable and sustainable future. And by making the decision to eat plant-based meals, we can help reduce the demand for animal products while also supporting the ethical treatment of animals.

Well-known health institutions, such as the British Dietetic Association and the American Dietetic Association, consider that a well-planned and balanced vegan diet provides all the essential nutrients required for optimum health, including protein. Whole plant foods such as legumes and whole grains provide fibre, promoting digestive health, as well as a variety of phytonutrients and antioxidants that contribute to overall health. As an additional benefit, these phytonutrients offer anti-inflammatory properties that can help reduce the risk of inflammatory diseases and aid post-exercise recovery.

WHAT ARE THE BENEFITS OF PLANT-BASED PROTEINS?

Plant-based proteins can help contribute to heart health by being low in saturated fat and free from cholesterol. Additionally, by switching from animal proteins to plant proteins, studies show a reduction in the risk of developing various lifestyle diseases such as heart disease, type 2 diabetes, obesity and other health conditions. Studies have also shown that plant proteins are just as effective as animal proteins in building muscle and supporting their repair and recovery.

A common concern among health-conscious people interested in the vegan diet is that not all plant-based foods contain all nine essential amino acids. While this is true for the most part, some high-protein foods do, including tofu, edamame beans, tempeh, soya milk, quinoa and hemp seeds. Some legumes, whole grains and vegetables do require combining with other plant-based foods to achieve a balanced amino acid profile, but this is as simple as pairing broccoli with rice in the same meal.

Consuming an array of high-quality plant-based proteins can help you to regulate your weight as well as support your overall health.

HOW MUCH PROTEIN DO YOU NEED?

The UK government recommends a protein intake of 35-45 g per day for women and 45–55 g per day for men. However, to calculate your daily requirement more accurately, multiply 0.8 g protein per kg body weight, so if you weighed 55 kg (121 lb), you would require 44 g protein per day, or if you weighed 75 kg (165 lb), you would require 60 g protein per day.

While anyone can follow a high-protein diet, particular groups such as athletes, those over the age of 60 and pregnant women will need more protein. If you want to follow a high-protein diet, you will need to aim for 1.2 g protein per kg of body weight, so if you weighed 55 kg (121 lb), you would need 66 g protein, or if you weighed 75 kg (165 lb), you would require 90 g protein per day.

PROTEIN-PACKED PLANT-BASED INGREDIENTS

Incorporating a variety of plant-based protein sources can help you achieve a well-balanced vegan diet. Plant proteins can be sourced from a wide range of foods, including legumes such as tofu, tempeh, lentils, chickpeas, edamame beans and black beans, whole grains such as quinoa, buckwheat and wholewheat, as well as nuts like cashews and seeds such as hemp seeds.

Many vegan meat alternatives also provide rich sources of plant-based protein, including plant-based mince, chicken pieces, bacon bits and vegan egg replacement, which all feature in the recipes and are now widely available to buy. By utilizing these products in conjunction with whole grains, legumes and vegetables, you can enjoy nutrition-packed, flavoursome meals that meet your protein needs while satisfying carnivorous appetites.

There are also many vegan protein powders available that can be easily incorporated into meals and snacks such as smoothies and bakes to boost protein effortlessly.

A combination of plant-based proteins consumed over the day will readily provide the necessary amino acids for the body and offer additional nutritional benefits. Legumes such as beans and lentils offer a good source of protein and are also rich in fibre to aid digestion and iron to prevent anaemia. Whole grains such as quinoa, besides being another great source of protein, also provide bioactive compounds that have anti-inflammatory and antioxidative effects.

If you can master vegan protein sources, you will be able to create delicious and nutritious high-protein meals any time and anywhere. To do this, first familiarize yourself with all the main plant protein sources, as well as staple plant-based ingredients, so that you can include them in your favourite meals and ensure a well-rounded nutritionally balanced diet. Then simply begin incorporating different protein sources in one dish, such as mixing lentils and quinoa together in a flavourful grain salad, or adding chickpeas and tofu to a stir-fry or cooked plant-based bacon bits to your side salad. Be creative and experiment with different flavours and textures to keep your meals interesting and packed with nutrition.

HIGH-PROTEIN VEGAN INGREDIENT SWAPS

When you initially start a high-protein vegan diet, making simple swaps in your meals is a helpful way to boost the protein content overall. It is also good to incorporate more high-protein foods and combine them to ensure you are eating enough calories

	FOOD	PROTEIN PER 100 G	SWAP FOR	PROTEIN PER 100 G
GRAINS	rice noodles (uncooked)	6 g	black bean noodles (uncooked)	44 g
	wholewheat pasta (uncooked)	13 g	chickpea pasta (uncooked)	22 g
	brown rice (uncooked)	7.5 g	lentils (uncooked)	24 g
	white rice (uncooked)	6.5 g	quinoa (uncooked)	14 g
NUTS & SEEDS	almond milk	0.5 g	high-protein soya milk	5 g
	flaxseeds	18 g	hemp seeds (hulled)	30 g
	coconut bacon (cooked)	3 g	plant-based (soya) bacon (cooked)	24 g
	cashew nuts	18 g	peanuts	26 g
	vegan butter	0.5 g	peanut butter	22 g
LEGUMES	chickpeas (canned/cooked)	7 g	tofu (cooked)	18 g
	black beans (canned/cooked)	6 g	tempeh (cooked)	20 g
	tofu (cooked)	18 g	plant-based chicken (cooked)	23 g
	kidney beans (canned/cooked)	5 g	plant-based mince (cooked)	17 g
	peas (cooked)	5 g	shelled edamame beans (cooked)	12 g

and getting a variety of amino acids, while also increasing the total protein content of your meals.

For example, a 50 g (2 oz) serving of black bean noodles contains 22 g protein, and when combined with a 100 g (3½ oz) serving of tempeh, your meal will contain 42 g protein, which is about half your daily intake. You can boost this even further by adding some broccoli and peanuts. How easy is that?

With that approach in mind, opposite are some high-protein swaps to consider.

ACHIEVING A BALANCED HIGH-PROTEIN VEGAN DIET

To ensure that your high-protein ingredients form part of a balanced and varied diet, they must be accompanied by adequate amounts of carbohydrates for energy (see below for advice on side dishes), healthy fats from nuts and seeds (see page 9) and micronutrients from fresh whole foods such as fruits and vegetables (see page 8). It is also essential to ensure other vital nutrients are included such as vitamin B12 and vitamin D, which can be sourced via supplements or fortified foods.

Recommended side dishes

To complement your high-protein meals, choose from these flavourful and nutritionally beneficial side serving options:

QUINOA as a side dish is a complete protein, as well as being a good source of fibre, iron and magnesium. A serving of around 185 g (6½ oz) cooked quinoa will provide 8 g protein, 5 g fibre, 25% of your daily zinc requirement, 37% magnesium and 39% copper. Quinoa can be served with various vegetables, nuts, fruits or legumes to create a flavourful and nutritious side dish.

BROWN RICE is an excellent side dish for both protein and complex carbohydrates, providing sustained energy. A 185 g (6½ oz) serving of cooked brown rice contains 5 g protein, alongside essential minerals such as 100% of your recommended daily intake of manganese, 37% vitamin B3 (niacin) and 25% magnesium. Swap brown rice for antioxidant-rich wild rice, red rice or black rice for more variety and additional health benefits.

SWEET POTATOES are high in vitamins, minerals and fibre, and can contribute complex carbohydrates to a balanced diet and support overall nutrition. Although a medium-sized sweet potato contains only about 3 g protein, it offers plenty of other nutritional value, supplying over 200% of your daily vitamin A requirement and 27% of your potassium needs. Roast sweet potatoes to enjoy hot or cold as a delicious and satisfying side dish.

BROCCOLI is a high-protein vegetable and perfect for serving as a side dish to a wide variety of meals. It is rich in vitamin C and vitamin K, providing 168% and 300% respectively of your daily requirement from a 315 g (11½ oz) serving. A 315 g (11½ oz) serving also provides almost 5 g protein, 6 g fibre and 20% of your daily omega-3 requirement. Serve broccoli steamed or add to stir-fries, salads and pasta dishes to boost their protein and nutritional value further.

WHOLEGRAIN BREAD is another great food to complement your meals, providing both protein and complex carbohydrates. A two-slice serving contains around 10 g protein, 5 g fibre and around 30% of the B vitamins niacin and thiamine. To add a satisfying crunch and extra nutrition to soups and stews, serve with toasted wholegrain bread.

EDAMAME BEANS offer an impressive 18 g complete plant protein per 160 g (5½ oz) serving. A 160 g (5½ oz) serving also contains 8 g fibre, 50% of your daily omega-3 requirement, 27% zinc and 20% iron. These beans are super versatile as a side dish and can be enjoyed boiled or roasted alongside stir-fries, salads, grain bowls, soups, curries and more for added protein and other nutritional value, as well as texture.

Essential nutrients & sources

When adopting a vegan diet, it is important to be aware of how incorporating a variety of foods can help you get all the essential nutrients you need. Most of these nutrients can be easily sourced from everyday plant-based foods and ingredients, although it may require a conscious effort to ensure adequate intakes, and it is advised to supplement with a good-quality multivitamin to ensure any dietary shortfalls are met. Certain age groups or pregnant women may require larger amounts of specific nutrients, so it is advisable to consult a professional for guidance.

These are the key nutrients you should pay special attention to and where best to source in a vegan diet:

VITAMIN B12 is essential to support energy levels and brain function. While it was historically common for vegans and vegetarians to be deficient in this nutrient, today it is easy to obtain from many staple fortified foods such as plant-based milk, cereals and nutritional yeast. However, it is still recommended to ensure that your daily multivitamin includes this vital nutrient.

VITAMIN D is required for our bodies to absorb calcium, as well as supporting bone health and immune function. It is primarily obtained through sun exposure, and some fortified foods contain it, such as plant-based milks or nutritional yeast. But in countries like the UK that are not blessed with adequate sunshine all year round, it is important to take it as a supplement.

IODINE is required to regulate thyroid function. Numerous foods contain iodine in trace amounts, but the best sources are sea vegetables, iodized salt or via a supplement.

CALCIUM is one of the main minerals required for developing strong bones and teeth. Good sources for vegans are fortified plant-based milks, leafy greens, some other vegetables such as broccoli and pak choy, legumes, tofu and plant-based yogurts.

IRON is another essential nutrient that women following a vegan diet in particular should focus on, as they lose iron during their monthly cycles. It is required for oxygenating the blood and for energy production. Iron is found abundantly in legumes, tofu, tempeh, fortified cereals, leafy greens, whole grains, nuts, seeds and dried fruits.

ZINC is an important mineral for immune function and metabolism, and is found in legumes, whole grains, nuts and seeds.

OMEGA-3 FATTY ACIDS are required for heart health and to support brain function. To gain your daily requirement easily, include flaxseeds, chia seeds, hemp seeds, walnuts or an algae supplement in your diet.

Healthy plant-based fats

Plant-based fats are mostly made up of monounsaturated, polyunsaturated and some saturated fats. These provide energy, support brain function and are necessary for the absorption of fat-soluble vitamins. Swapping animal fats for plant-based fats can have significant health benefits.

Including a range of plant-based fats in your vegan diet can help ensure that you are getting the necessary nutrients to support your energy levels, metabolism and general health, and the meal plans (see pages 10–13) and recipes in this book do just that.

It is recommended to have no more than 30 g saturated fat per day on average, as these fats can be harmful in larger amounts, and research has shown that diets high in saturated fats increase the risk of chronic diseases such as obesity, heart disease and type 2 diabetes. Foods that contain high amounts of saturated fat include meat, dairy, eggs, processed foods and oils. However, with the rise of processed foods now suitable for vegans, and with many containing high amounts of saturated fats, these foods can also compromise health. They include ready-made pizzas, cakes,

biscuits, pastries, meat alternatives such as plant-based burgers, mince and sausages, vegan butter and coconut yogurt.

Plant-based diets that are centred around whole foods provide healthy fats that can reduce the risk of chronic disease, so it is best to include fewer processed foods and replace them in moderation with the foods listed below. Remember to soak nuts and seeds before eating or using to make them more digestible and allow your body to absorb more of their valuable nutrition.

NUTS

Almonds	Coconut
Cashew nuts	Pistachio nuts
Walnuts	Peanuts

SEEDS

Sunflower seeds	Chia seeds
Pumpkin seeds	Hemp seeds
Flaxseeds	Poppy seeds

OILS

Olive oil	Flaxseed oil
Sesame oil	Vegetable oil
Avocado oil	

OTHER OIL-RICH FOODS

Avocados	Coconut yogurt
Olives	Tofu

Weekly Meal Plans

These two meal plans have been specially devised for a high-protein vegan diet based on the recipes in the book, one for those following a 2,000-calorie daily diet and another for those following a 2,500-calorie daily diet. It is recommended that women following a 2,000-calorie high-protein vegan diet aim for 75-85 g protein per day, while men following a 2,500-calorie diet aim for 95–105 g protein per day. This has been determined to meet the protein requirements for optimal health and to support physical activity levels.

The meal plans provide a variety of plant-based protein sources to help you achieve your daily protein needs and to ensure a balanced diet. It is recommended to include a multivitamin that covers your vitamin B12, vitamin D and iodine daily requirements.

2,000 KCAL

MONDAY

Breakfast	Mango & Orange Smoothie	1 serving (281 g)
Lunch	Creamy Vegan Tuna & Leek Pasta	1 serving (305 g)
Snack	Griddled Greek-style Sandwiches	1 serving (238 g)
Dinner	'Meaty' Boston Beans	1 serving (330 g)
Dessert	Apple Fritters with Blackberry Sauce	1 serving (338 g)
Supplements	Multivitamin supplement	

TUESDAY

Breakfast	Fruit & Nut Bars	1 bar (86 g)
Lunch	Tikka Lentil Koftas	1 serving (391 g)
Snack	Double Berry Muffins	1 muffin (85 g)
Dinner	Chilli Tacos	1 serving (602 g)
Dessert	Frosted Banana Bars	1 bar (93 g)
Supplements	Multivitamin supplement	

WEDNESDAY

Breakfast	Potato Bread with Tomatoes	1 serving (248 g)
Lunch	Chunky Tomato & Bean Stew	1 serving (597 g)
Snack	Chocolate Yum Yums	1 square (38 g)
Dinner	Spicy Chickpea Curry	1 serving (451 g)
Dessert	Peanut Butter Cookies	1 cookie (50 g)
Supplements	Multivitamin supplement	

THURSDAY

Breakfast	Mushroom Tofu Scramble	1 serving (370 g)
Lunch	Flatbread, Roasted Veg & Hummus	1 serving (317 g)
Snack	Asparagus Frittata	1 serving (240 g)
Dinner	Delicatessen Pasta	1 serving (237 g)
Dessert	Frosted Banana Bars	1 bar (93 g)
Supplements	Multivitamin supplement	

FRIDAY

Breakfast	Maple Granola	1 serving (394 g)
Lunch	Mediterranean Beans	1 serving (252 g)
Snack	Chocolate Yum Yums	1 square (38 g)
Dinner	Spicy Bean Burgers	1 serving (452 g)
Dessert	Peanut Butter Cookies	1 cookie (50 g)
Supplements	Multivitamin supplement	

SATURDAY

Breakfast	Chickpea & Spinach Omelette	1 serving (315 g)
Lunch	Puy Lentil & Butter Bean Salad	1 serving (332 g)
Snack	Cheat's Pepper Pizza	1 serving (161 g)
Dinner	Pad Thai	1 serving (291 g)
Dessert	Spiced Pear & Cranberry Muffins	1 muffin (111 g)
Supplements	Multivitamin supplement	

SUNDAY

Breakfast	Blueberry & Banana French Toast	1 serving (188 g)
Lunch	Marinated Tofu with Vegetables	1 serving (447 g)
Snack	Griddled Greek-style Sandwiches	1 serving (238 g)
Dinner	Veggie Sausage Hotpot	1 serving (433 g)
Dessert	Spiced Pear & Cranberry Muffins	1 muffin (111 g)
Supplements	Multivitamin supplement	

MONDAY

Breakfast	Toasted Muesli with Coconut Chips	1 serving (434 g)
Snack 1	Plant-based Mince & Courgette Koftas	1 serving (213 g)
Lunch	Lentil, Mustard & Chickpea Soup	1 serving (384 g)
Snack 2	Borlotti Bean & Pepper Bruschetta	1 serving (252 g)
Dinner	Lentil Bolognese	1 serving (520 g)
Dessert	Warm Pecan Caramel Cupcakes	1 cupcake (81 g)
Supplements	Multivitamin supplement	

TUESDAY

Breakfast	Quinoa Porridge with Raspberries	1 serving (463 g)
Snack 1	Power Bars	1 bar (75 g)
Lunch	Spicy Edamame Bean & Noodle Salad	1 serving (178 g)
Snack 2	Borlotti Bean & Pepper Bruschetta	1 serving (252 g)
Dinner	Coconut Dahl with Toasted Naan Fingers	1 serving (322 g)
Dessert	Rice Pudding with Drunken Raisins	1 serving (199 g)
Supplements	Multivitamin supplement	

WEDNESDAY

Breakfast	Home-baked Beans on Toast	1 serving (378 g)
Snack 1	Plant-based Mince & Courgette Koftas	1 serving (213 g)
Lunch	Chilli & Courgette Penne	1 serving (324 g)
Snack 2	Apricot & Sunflower Muffins	1 muffin (88 g)
Dinner	Spicy Bean Burgers	1 serving (452 g)
Dessert	Jam Roly-poly	1 serving (178 g)
Supplements	Multivitamin supplement	

THURSDAY

Breakfast	Mixed Berry Smoothie	1 serving (364 g)
Snack 1	Power Bars	1 bar (75 g)
Lunch	Puy Lentil Stew with Garlic Bread	1 serving (506 g)
Snack 2	Banana & Sultana Drop Scones	3 scones (166 g)
Dinner	Vegan Bacon, Chorizo & Tomato Linguine	1 serving (482 g)
Dessert	Steamed Pudding with Mango	1 serving (142 g)
Supplements	Multivitamin supplement	

FRIDAY

Breakfast	Creamy Mushrooms with Walnuts	1 serving (288 g)
Snack 1	Plant-based Mince & Courgette Koftas	1 serving (213 g)
Lunch	Tofu With Pak Choi & Spring Onions	1 serving (484 g)
Snack 2	Banana & Sultana Drop Scones	3 scones (166 g)
Dinner	Chilli Sin Carne	1 serving (755 g)
Dessert	Jam Roly-poly	1 serving (178 g)
Supplements	Multivitamin supplement	

SATURDAY

Breakfast	Toffee & Banana Pancakes	1 serving (262 g)
Snack 1	Plant-based Mince & Courgette Koftas	1 serving (213 g)
Lunch	Edamame & Pesto Soup	1 serving (471 g)
Snack 2	Apricot & Sunflower Muffins	1 muffin (88 g)
Dinner	Spinach, Tomato & Tofu Curry	1 serving (421 g)
Dessert	Steamed Pudding with Mango	1 serving (142 g)
Supplements	Multivitamin supplement	

SUNDAY

Breakfast	Plant-based Sausage & Sweet Potato Hash	1 serving (353 g)
Snack 1	Power Bars	1 bar (75 g)
Lunch	Quick Quesadillas	1 serving (312 g)
Snack 2	Chickpea, Tomato & Pepper Salad	1 serving (474 g)
Dinner	Meat-free Cottage Pie	1 serving (536 g)
Dessert	Warm Pecan Caramel Cupcakes	1 cupcake (81 g)
Supplements	Multivitamin supplement	

Power Breakfasts

Blueberry & Banana French Toast

15 MINUTES					
4 SERVINGS	371	KCAL / SERVING	4 G	FIBRE	
	11 G	PROTEIN	16 G	SUGAR	
	15 G	FAT	6 G	SAT FAT	
	50 G	CARBS	401 MG	SODIUM	

90 g (3¼ oz) liquid vegan egg replacement

4 tablespoons soya milk

4 teaspoons caster sugar

4 slices of crusty white bread

50 g (2 oz) vegan butter

50 g (2 oz) blueberries

2 bananas, sliced

TO SERVE (OPTIONAL)

soya or oat cream

maple syrup

Beat together the egg replacement, soya milk and 2 teaspoons of the caster sugar in a bowl. Pour into a shallow dish and dip both sides of the bread slices into the egg replacement mixture.

Heat the vegan butter in a large frying pan, add the bread (you might need to cook 1 or 2 slices at a time) and cook for 2 minutes on each side until crisp and golden. Sprinkle over the remaining sugar.

Cut the French toasts in half diagonally and scatter with the blueberries and banana slices. Serve with soya or oat cream and drizzle over a little maple syrup, if liked.

For Blueberry Pancakes with Banana

Put 75 g (3 oz) self-raising flour, 1 tablespoon caster sugar, 45 g (1½ oz) liquid vegan egg replacement and 75 ml (3 fl oz) soya milk in a blender or food processor and blend together to make a smooth thick batter. Stir in 25 g (1 oz) blueberries. Heat 1 tablespoon sunflower oil in a large frying pan, add 2 large spoonfuls of the batter and cook for 1–2 minutes on each side until golden. Repeat with the remaining batter to make another 2 pancakes. Serve warm with the sliced bananas and a drizzle of maple syrup as above.

Chickpea & Spinach Omelette

30 MINUTES		
4 SERVINGS		

468	KCAL / SERVING	9 G	FIBRE
15 G	PROTEIN	7 G	SUGAR
29 G	FAT	11 G	SAT FAT
40 G	CARBS	831 MG	SODIUM

2 tablespoons olive oil

1 large onion, sliced

1 red pepper, cored, deseeded
    and sliced

½ teaspoon hot smoked or
    sweet paprika

400 g (13 oz) can chickpeas, rinsed
    and drained

100 g (3½ oz) spinach leaves, rinsed,
    drained and roughly sliced

225 g (7½ oz) liquid vegan egg
    replacement

75 g (3 oz) pitted green olives,
    roughly chopped

150 g (5 oz) Cheddar-style vegan
    cheese, grated

salt and pepper

Heat the olive oil in a large nonstick frying pan. Add the onion and red pepper and cook gently for 7–8 minutes until soft and golden. Stir in the salt and pepper , paprika and chickpeas, then cook for 1 minute, stirring frequently. Add the spinach leaves and cook until just wilted.

Pour the egg replacement into the pan and cook gently, without stirring, for 4–5 minutes until almost set.

Sprinkle with the olives and vegan cheese, then cook under a preheated hot grill, keeping the handle away from the heat, for 4–5 minutes until golden and set. Slice into wedges and serve immediately.

For Mushroom & Black Bean Omelette

Follow the recipe above, swapping the red pepper for 125 g (4 oz) chestnut or button mushrooms, trimmed and sliced, and the chickpeas for a 400 g (13 oz) can black beans, rinsed and drained.

Creamy Mushrooms with Walnuts

20 MINUTES				
2 SERVINGS	586	KCAL / SERVING	7 G	FIBRE
	18 G	PROTEIN	9 G	SUGAR
	32 G	FAT	3 G	SAT FAT
	60 G	CARBS	584 MG	SODIUM

1 tablespoon olive oil

150 g (5 oz) chestnut mushrooms, trimmed and sliced

1 garlic clove, crushed

leaves from 2 thyme sprigs, plus extra sprigs to garnish

150 ml (¼ pint) soya or oat cream

1 teaspoon soy sauce

50 g (2 oz) chopped walnuts, toasted

pepper

2 bagels, halved and toasted, to serve

Heat the olive oil in a frying pan, add the mushrooms and cook over a high heat, stirring frequently, for 2 minutes until browned and softened.

Reduce the heat and add the garlic, thyme leaves, soya or oat cream and soy sauce. Simmer, stirring, for 3 minutes, adding a little water if the sauce is too thick. Stir in the walnuts and season with pepper (the soy sauce is salty, so you won't need to season with salt).

Spoon the mushroom mixture over the toasted bagels and garnish with thyme sprigs before serving.

Fruit & Nut Bars

25 MINUTES

8 SERVINGS

336	KCAL / BAR	4 G	FIBRE
7 G	PROTEIN	18 G	SUGAR
16 G	FAT	6 G	SAT FAT
43 G	CARBS	41 MG	SODIUM

100 g (3½ oz) vegan butter, plus
  extra for greasing

4 tablespoons maple syrup

2 tablespoons soft light brown sugar

150 g (5 oz) jumbo oats

100 g (3½ oz) porridge oats

50 g (2 oz) mixed nuts, chopped

150 g (5 oz) mixed pitted soft
  dried fruit, such as figs, dates,
  ready-to-eat apricots and
  cranberries, chopped

2 tablespoons sunflower seeds

Grease a 20 cm (8 inch) square nonstick baking tin lightly and line the base with nonstick baking paper.

Melt the vegan butter, maple syrup and sugar together in a saucepan. Stir in all the remaining ingredients except the sunflower seeds, then press the mixture into the prepared tin.

Sprinkle over the sunflower seeds and bake in a preheated oven, 200°C (400°F), Gas Mark 6, for 15 minutes or until golden. Cut into 8 bars and leave to cool completely in the tin. Remove the bars and peel off the paper. Store any remaining bars in an airtight container for up to 3 days.

Home-baked Beans on Toast

1½ HOURS, PLUS SOAKING			
4 SERVINGS			

513	KCAL / SERVING	6 G	FIBRE
27 G	PROTEIN	18 G	SUGAR
10 G	FAT	1 G	SAT FAT
83 G	CARBS	1659 MG	SODIUM

350 g (11½ oz) dried haricot beans

2 tablespoons rapeseed oil

1 red onion, cut into wedges

400 g (13 oz) can chopped tomatoes

2 tablespoons tomato purée

2 tablespoons dark muscovado sugar

3 tablespoons vegan red wine vinegar

1 teaspoon paprika

1 teaspoon mustard powder

275 ml (9 fl oz) vegan vegetable stock

salt and pepper

4 slices of wholemeal bread, toasted, to serve

2 tablespoons chopped flat leaf parsley, to garnish

Soak the dried beans in plenty of cold water overnight.

Drain the beans, put in a saucepan and cover with cold water. Bring to the boil, then drain and return to the pan. Cover with fresh cold water, bring to the boil and boil for 10 minutes, then cover and simmer for 50 minutes until tender.

Meanwhile, heat the rapeseed oil in a separate saucepan, add the onion and cook for 3 minutes until it is just starting to soften. Add the tomatoes, tomato purée, sugar, vinegar, paprika, mustard powder and stock. Bring to the boil, stirring, then reduce the heat and simmer, uncovered, for 20 minutes until it has reduced slightly.

Drain the cooked beans and add to the tomato sauce. Simmer for a further 15–20 minutes, covered, until thick, then season with salt and pepper. Serve on the toasted wholemeal bread, scattered with the chopped parsley.

For Quick Chilli Beans with Vegan Sausages

Heat a 400 g (13 oz) can chopped tomatoes in a saucepan with 2 tablespoons each tomato purée and dark muscovado sugar, 1 tablespoon sweet chilli sauce and 1 chopped red chilli. Bring to the boil, stirring, then simmer, uncovered, for 10 minutes. Add a rinsed and drained 400 g (13 oz) can haricot beans and simmer for a further 10 minutes. Meanwhile, cook 300 g (10 oz) plant-based sausages under a preheated medium grill or in a splash of sunflower oil in a frying pan, turning frequently, for about 15 minutes until evenly browned and cooked through. Cut into chunks and stir into the bean mixture.

Mango & Orange Smoothie

5 MINUTES

2 SERVINGS

170	KCAL / SERVING	2 G	FIBRE
5 G	PROTEIN	23 G	SUGAR
3 G	FAT	0 G	SAT FAT
34 G	CARBS	5 MG	SODIUM

1 ripe mango, peeled, stoned and chopped, or 150 g (5 oz) frozen mango chunks

2 tablespoons natural soya yogurt

150 ml (¼ pint) high-protein soya milk

150 ml (¼ pint) orange juice

finely grated zest and juice of 1 lime

2 teaspoons agave nectar, or to taste

Blend all the ingredients together in a blender or food processor until smooth.

Pour into 2 glasses and serve immediately.

For Lemon & Mango Smoothie

Blend together 150 g (5 oz) mango flesh, 2 tablespoons porridge oats, 2 tablespoons natural soya yogurt, the finely grated zest and juice of ½ lemon and 150 ml (¼ pint) high-protein soya milk in a blender or food processor until smooth. Sweeten to taste with agave nectar. Pour into 2 glasses and serve.

Mushroom Tofu Scramble

15		490	KCAL / SERVING	2 G	FIBRE
MINUTES		27 G	PROTEIN	6 G	SUGAR
2		33 G	FAT	5 G	SAT FAT
SERVINGS		25 G	CARBS	861 MG	SODIUM

2 tablespoons rapeseed or olive oil

200 g (7 oz) chestnut mushrooms, trimmed and quartered

250 g (8 oz) firm tofu, drained, patted dry and crumbled

125 g (4 oz) cherry tomatoes

1 tablespoon mushroom ketchup

3 tablespoons chopped flat leaf parsley

salt and pepper

2 baked hash browns, to serve

Heat the oil in a frying pan, add the mushrooms and cook over a high heat, stirring frequently, for 2 minutes until browned and softened. Add the tofu and cook, stirring, for 1 minute.

Add the tomatoes to the pan and cook for 2 minutes until starting to soften. Stir in the mushroom ketchup and half the parsley, then season with salt and pepper.

Serve immediately with the hash browns, sprinkled with the remaining parsley.

For 5 g more protein, swap the hash browns for one slice of wholemeal sourdough bread per serving.

For Spinach & Sweetcorn Tofu Scramble

Heat 2 tablespoons rapeseed or olive oil in a frying pan. Add 250 g (8 oz) drained, patted dry and crumbled firm tofu with 1 teaspoon smoked paprika and cook, stirring, for 2 minutes until hot. Add 75 g (3 oz) frozen or drained canned sweetcorn kernels and heat through for 1 minute, then add 250 g (8 oz) spinach leaves and heat until just wilted. Season with salt and pepper and serve.

Potato Bread with Tomatoes

1½
HOURS, PLUS
RISING AND
COOLING

4
SERVINGS

438	KCAL / SERVING	7 G	FIBRE
12 G	PROTEIN	4 G	SUGAR
12 G	FAT	2 G	SAT FAT
77 G	CARBS	594 MG	SODIUM

375 g (12 oz) potatoes, peeled

1 teaspoon fast-action dried yeast

1 teaspoon caster sugar

1 tablespoon sunflower oil, plus extra
   for oiling

200 g (7 oz) strong white bread flour,
   plus extra for dusting

100 g (3½ oz) strong wholemeal
   bread flour

2 tablespoons chopped rosemary

1 tablespoon thyme leaves

salt and pepper

TOMATO TOPPING

2 tablespoons olive oil

250 g (8 oz) mixed-coloured baby
   tomatoes, halved

½ teaspoon thyme leaves

½ teaspoon sea salt flakes

*For 8 g more protein per serving,
swap the tomatoes for tofu
scramble. To make the scramble,
crumble 200 g (7 oz) drained
and patted dry firm tofu into a
frying pan and heat through with
¼ teaspoon ground turmeric and
a pinch each of salt and pepper.* →

Cook the potatoes in a large saucepan of lightly salted boiling water for 15–20 minutes until tender but not flaky. Drain really well, reserving the cooking liquid.

Place 6 tablespoons of the potato cooking liquid in a large bowl and leave to cool until lukewarm. Sprinkle over the yeast, then stir in the sugar and set aside for 10 minutes.

Mash the potatoes with the sunflower oil, then stir into the yeast mixture and mix well with a wooden spoon. Mix in the flours, herbs and some salt and pepper, then turn out on to a lightly floured surface and knead well to incorporate the last of the flour. Knead the dough until soft and pliable, then place in a lightly oiled bowl, cover with clingfilm and leave to rise in a warm place for 1 hour until well risen.

Knead the dough on a lightly floured surface, then roughly shape into a round, place on a baking sheet and lightly cover with oiled clingfilm. Leave to prove in a warm place for 30 minutes. Score a cross in the dough with a knife and bake in a preheated oven, 220°C (425°F), Gas Mark 7, for 35–40 minutes until well risen and crusty on top. Transfer to a wire rack to cool for 30 minutes.

Cut 4 slices of the bread and lightly toast. Meanwhile, for the topping, heat the olive oil in a frying pan, add the tomatoes and cook over a high heat for 2–3 minutes until softened. Stir in the thyme and salt flakes. Serve with the toasted bread, seasoned with pepper.

Maple Granola

40 MINUTES, PLUS COOLING			
4 SERVINGS			

617	KCAL / SERVING	10 G	FIBRE
21 G	PROTEIN	18 G	SUGAR
30 G	FAT	2 G	SAT FAT
70 G	CARBS	7 MG	SODIUM

5 tablespoons maple syrup

2 tablespoons sunflower oil

250 g (8 oz) porridge oats

50 g (2 oz) hazelnuts, roughly chopped

50 g (2 oz) blanched almonds,
   roughly chopped

50 g (2 oz) dried cranberries

50 g (2 oz) dried blueberries

TO SERVE (PER SERVING)

250 ml (8 fl oz) soya milk

yogurt and fresh fruit (optional)

Heat the maple syrup and sunflower oil together gently in a small saucepan.

Mix the oats and nuts together thoroughly in a large bowl. Pour over the warm syrup mixture and stir well to combine.

Spread the mixture over a large nonstick baking sheet and bake in a preheated oven, 150°C (300°F), Gas Mark 2, for 20–25 minutes, stirring halfway through, until golden.

Leave to cool completely, then stir in the dried berries. Serve with soya milk, or with yogurt and fresh fruit, if liked. Any remaining granola can be stored in an airtight container.

For 4 g more protein per serving, swap the regular soya milk for high-protein soya milk.

For Oven-baked Chocolate, Almond & Cherry Granola

Stir 2 tablespoons sifted cocoa powder into the warmed syrup and sunflower oil mixture as above. Mix the porridge oats and 100 g (3½ oz) blanched almonds together in a large bowl. Pour over the warm cocoa and syrup mixture and stir well to combine. Bake as above and leave to cool, then stir in 100 g (3½ oz) dried cherries. Serve with high-protein soya milk.

Toffee & Banana Pancakes

25 MINUTES			
4 SERVINGS			

500	KCAL / SERVING	2 G	FIBRE
10 G	PROTEIN	26 G	SUGAR
28 G	FAT	7 G	SAT FAT
53 G	CARBS	110 MG	SODIUM

100 g (3½ oz) plain flour

pinch of salt

45 g (1¾ oz) liquid vegan egg
   replacement

300 ml (½ pint) soya milk

2–3 tablespoons sunflower oil

2 bananas, sliced

TOFFEE SAUCE

50 g (2 oz) unsalted vegan butter

50 g (2 oz) light muscovado sugar

2 tablespoons golden syrup

150 ml (¼ pint) plant-based
   double cream

*For 20 g more protein per
serving, add 33 g (1¼ oz) or
1 scoop vegan protein powder to
the pancake batter.* ⟶

Sift the flour into a bowl and stir in the salt. Add the egg replacement, then gradually whisk in the soya milk to make a smooth batter. Set aside.

For the toffee sauce, put the vegan butter, sugar and golden syrup in a small saucepan and heat gently until the butter has melted and the sugar dissolves, stirring occasionally. Bring to the boil and cook for 3–4 minutes until just beginning to darken around the edges.

Remove the pan from the heat, then gradually pour in the plant-based cream. Tilt the pan to mix and, as the bubbles subside, stir with a wooden spoon. Set aside.

Heat the sunflower oil in an 18 cm (7 inch) frying pan, then pour off the excess into a small bowl. Pour a little pancake batter over the base of the pan, tilt the pan to coat the base evenly with batter and cook for 2 minutes until the underside is golden. Loosen with a spatula, turn over and cook the second side in the same way. Slide on to a plate and keep warm in a preheated oven, 160°C (325°F), Gas Mark 3, while you repeat with the remaining batter, adding more of the oil to the pan as needed.

Fold the pancakes and arrange on serving plates. Top with the banana slices and drizzle with the toffee sauce.

Mixed Berry Smoothie

5 MINUTES			
2 SERVINGS			

274	KCAL / SERVING	4 G	FIBRE
18 G	PROTEIN	25 G	SUGAR
5 G	FAT	0 G	SAT FAT
41 G	CARBS	17 MG	SODIUM

1 small ripe banana, roughly chopped

175 g (6 oz) mixed berries, such
   as raspberries, blueberries
   and strawberries

250 ml (8 fl oz) vanilla soya yogurt

150 ml (¼ pint) soya milk

33 g (1¼ oz) or 1 scoop vegan
   protein powder

Blend all the ingredients together in a blender or food processor until thick and smooth, adding a little more soya milk if you prefer a thinner consistency.

Pour the smoothie into 2 glasses and serve immediately.

For High-protein Strawberry Oat Smoothie

Blend together ½ roughly chopped ripe banana or mango and 2 tablespoons porridge oats in a blender or food processor until well combined. Add 300 ml (½ pint) soya milk and 33 g (1½ oz) or 1 scoop vanilla vegan protein powder and blend until smooth. Pour the smoothie into 2 glasses and serve immediately.

Quinoa Porridge with Raspberries

25 MINUTES				
2 SERVINGS	521	KCAL / SERVING	9 G	FIBRE
	22 G	PROTEIN	30 G	SUGAR
	16 G	FAT	1 G	SAT FAT
	74 G	CARBS	6 MG	SODIUM

600 ml (1 pint) soya milk

100 g (3½ oz) quinoa, rinsed and drained

2 tablespoons caster sugar

½ teaspoon ground cinnamon

125 g (4 oz) raspberries

1 tablespoon hulled hemp seeds

1 tablespoon mixed seeds, such as sunflower, flaxseeds and pumpkin

2 tablespoons maple syrup

Bring the soya milk to the boil in a small saucepan. Add the quinoa and return to the boil. Reduce the heat to low, cover and simmer for about 15 minutes until three-quarters of the milk has been absorbed.

Stir the sugar and cinnamon into the pan, re-cover and cook for 8–10 minutes or until almost all the milk has been absorbed and the quinoa is tender.

Spoon the porridge into 2 bowls, then top with the raspberries, sprinkle over the seeds and drizzle with the maple syrup. Serve immediately.

For 7 g more protein per serving, swap the regular soya milk for high-protein soya milk, and instead of mixed seeds, use only hemp seeds.

For Quinoa Porridge with Caramelized Banana

Cook the quinoa porridge as above. Meanwhile, in place of the raspberries, spray a nonstick frying pan with sunflower oil spray and cook 1 small sliced banana for 2–3 minutes on each side until golden brown. Drizzle with the maple syrup and serve on top of the quinoa porridge, sprinkled with the mixed seeds as above.

Plant-based Sausage & Sweet Potato Hash

45 MINUTES				
4 SERVINGS				

451	KCAL / SERVING	8 G	FIBRE
14 G	PROTEIN	14 G	SUGAR
24 G	FAT	3 G	SAT FAT
47 G	CARBS	65 MG	SODIUM

3 tablespoons olive oil

8 pork-flavour plant-based sausages

3 large red onions, thinly sliced

1 teaspoon caster sugar

500 g (1 lb) sweet potatoes, scrubbed
    and cut into small chunks

8 sage leaves

2 tablespoons balsamic vinegar

salt and pepper

Heat the olive oil in a large frying pan or flameproof casserole and fry the sausages, turning frequently, for about 10 minutes until browned all over. Drain to a plate.

Add the onions and sugar to the pan and cook gently, stirring frequently, until lightly browned. Return the sausages to the pan with the sweet potatoes, sage leaves and a little salt and pepper.

Cover the pan with a lid or foil and cook over a very gentle heat for about 25 minutes until the potatoes are tender.

Drizzle with the vinegar and check the seasoning before serving.

For 8 g more protein, serve with 1 thick slice of toasted bread per serving.

Toasted Muesli with Coconut Chips

633	KCAL / SERVING	11 G	FIBRE
25 G	PROTEIN	24 G	SUGAR
35 G	FAT	5 G	SAT FAT
59 G	CARBS	11 MG	SODIUM

30 MINUTES, PLUS COOLING

12 SERVINGS

350 g (11½ oz) porridge oats

75 g (3 oz) coconut chips

75 g (3 oz) sunflower seeds

200 g (7 oz) pumpkin seeds

150 g (5 oz) flaked almonds

100 g (3½ oz) hazelnuts

4 tablespoons maple syrup

2 tablespoons sunflower oil

250 g (8 oz) sultanas

75 g (3 oz) dried figs, roughly chopped

TO SERVE (PER SERVING)

250 ml (8 fl oz) soya milk

55 g (2¼ oz) raspberries

Mix together the oats, coconut chips, sunflower and pumpkin seeds, flaked almonds and hazelnuts in a large bowl. Transfer half the muesli mixture to a separate bowl and set aside.

Mix the maple syrup and sunflower oil together in a small bowl, then pour over the remaining half of the muesli and toss really well to lightly coat all the ingredients.

Line a large roasting tin with nonstick baking paper, scatter over the syrup-coated muesli and spread out in a single layer. Bake in a preheated oven, 150°C (300°F), Gas Mark 2, for 15–20 minutes, stirring occasionally, until golden and crisp.

Leave to cool completely, then toss with the uncooked muesli and the dried fruit. Store in an airtight container. Serve with soya milk and raspberries, if liked.

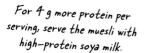

For 4 g more protein per serving, serve the muesli with high-protein soya milk.

For Soft Cinnamon Muesli with Almonds & Banana

Mix together 350 g (11½ oz) porridge oats, 250 g (8 oz) sultanas, 200 g (7 oz) each pumpkin seeds and toasted blanched almonds, 100 g (3½ oz) soft dried banana slices, 75 g (3 oz) each pitted dried dates and sunflower seeds and 2 teaspoons ground cinnamon in a large bowl. Store in airtight storage jars. Serve as above with soya milk (or soya yogurt) and fresh fruit, if liked.

Snacks & Quick Bites

Apricot & Sunflower Muffins

40 MINUTES				
12 SERVINGS	211	KCAL / MUFFIN	3 G	FIBRE
	5 G	PROTEIN	15 G	SUGAR
	6 G	FAT	1 G	SAT FAT
	35 G	CARBS	87 MG	SODIUM

300 g (10 oz) self-raising
 wholemeal flour

1 teaspoon baking powder

150 g (5 oz) light muscovado sugar

finely grated zest of 1 orange

200 ml (7 fl oz) plant-based crème
 fraîche or natural yogurt

135 g (4½ oz) liquid vegan egg
 replacement

225 g (7½ oz) can apricot halves in
 natural juice, drained and roughly
 chopped, juice reserved

3 tablespoons sunflower seeds

Line a deep 12-cup muffin tin with paper muffin cases.

Mix together the flour, baking powder, sugar and orange zest in a large bowl. In a separate bowl, mix together the plant-based crème fraîche or yogurt and egg replacement. Add to the flour mixture with the chopped apricots and mix together with a fork until only just combined, adding 2–3 tablespoons of the reserved canned apricot juice to make a soft, spoonable consistency.

Divide the mixture between the muffin cases and sprinkle with the sunflower seeds. Bake in a preheated oven, 200°C (400°F), Gas Mark 6, for 15–18 minutes until the muffins are well risen and the tops are cracked and golden brown. Leave to cool in the tin for 5 minutes, then transfer to a wire rack. Serve warm or cold.

For Peach & Orange Muffins

Make the muffin mixture as above, adding the diced flesh of 1 large peach, the finely grated zest of 1 orange and 2–3 tablespoons orange juice instead of the canned apricots and their juice. Bake and serve as above.

Banana & Sultana Drop Scones

105	KCAL / SCONE	1 G	FIBRE
3 G	PROTEIN	9 G	SUGAR
2 G	FAT	0 G	SAT FAT
20 G	CARBS	129 MG	SODIUM

25 MINUTES

10 SCONES

125 g (4 oz) self-raising flour

2 tablespoons caster sugar

½ teaspoon baking powder

1 small ripe banana, about 125 g (4 oz) with skin on, peeled and roughly mashed

45 g (1¾ oz) liquid vegan egg replacement

150 ml (¼ pint) soya milk

50 g (2 oz) sultanas

sunflower oil, for greasing

1 tablespoon golden or maple syrup, to serve

Mix together the flour, sugar and baking powder in a bowl. Add the mashed banana and egg replacement, then gradually whisk in the soya milk with a fork to make a smooth thick batter. Stir in the sultanas.

Pour a little sunflower oil on to a piece of folded kitchen paper and use to grease a griddle pan or heavy nonstick frying pan. Heat the pan, then drop in tablespoonfuls of the batter, well spaced apart. Cook for 2 minutes until bubbles appear on the top and the undersides are golden. Turn over and cook for a further 1–2 minutes until the second side is done. Repeat with the remaining batter.

Serve warm, topped with the golden or maple syrup. These are best eaten on the day they are made.

For 2 g more protein per scone, mix 28 g (1 oz) of your favourite vegan protein powder into the batter. You may need to add a splash more soya milk if the batter is too thick.

For Summer Berry Drop Scones

Make the batter as above, stirring in 125 g (4 oz) mixed blueberries and raspberries instead of the sultanas, then mix in 33 g (1½ oz) or 1 scoop vegan protein powder. Cook as above.

Chocolate Yum Yums

206	KCAL / SQUARE	2 G	FIBRE
4 G	PROTEIN	9 G	SUGAR
14 G	FAT	5 G	SAT FAT
18 G	CARBS	88 MG	SODIUM

20 MINUTES, PLUS COOLING

15 SERVINGS

150 g (5 oz) vegan plain dark chocolate, broken into pieces

100 g (3½ oz) crunchy peanut butter

25 g (1 oz) vegan butter

2 tablespoons golden syrup

150 g (5 oz) digestive biscuits

50 g (2 oz) almonds or cashew nuts

70 g (2¾ oz) sugared almonds, roughly chopped, to decorate

Line a shallow 20 cm (8 inch) square cake tin with nonstick baking paper.

Put the chocolate, peanut butter, vegan butter and golden syrup in a large saucepan and heat gently until melted, stirring occasionally. Remove the pan from the heat.

Place the digestives in a plastic bag and crush roughly using a rolling pin. Stir the crushed biscuits and the almonds or cashew nuts into the chocolate mixture and stir until evenly coated.

Spoon the mixture into the lined tin and level the surface. Chill in the refrigerator for 4 hours until firm.

Lift the cake out of the tin using the lining paper, cut into 15 small squares and peel off the paper. Decorate with the sugared almonds. Store in an airtight container for up to 3 days.

For High-protein Rocky Road

Melt 150 g (5 oz) vegan plain dark chocolate, broken into pieces, with 6 tablespoons crunchy peanut butter in a heatproof bowl set over a pan of barely simmering water. Remove the bowl from the pan and add 90 g (3¼ oz) vegan chocolate protein powder and 4 tablespoons liquid sweetener of your choice, then stir in 25 g (1 oz) each mini vegan marshmallows, crispy cereal, nuts or seeds and dried fruit. Transfer the mixture to the lined square cake tin and chill until firm, then cut into 15 small squares and store as above.

Double Berry Muffins

30 MINUTES				
12 SERVINGS	229	KCAL / MUFFIN	1 G	FIBRE
	5 G	PROTEIN	12 G	SUGAR
	9 G	FAT	2 G	SAT FAT
	33 G	CARBS	163 MG	SODIUM

300 g (10 oz) plain flour

3 teaspoons baking powder

125 g (4 oz) caster sugar

150 ml (¼ pint) natural soya yogurt

135 g (4½ oz) liquid vegan egg replacement

50 g (2 oz) salted vegan butter, melted

4 tablespoons sunflower oil

1½ teaspoons vanilla extract

100 g (3½ oz) blueberries

100 g (3½ oz) raspberries

Line a 12-cup muffin tin with paper muffin cases.

Mix together the flour, baking powder and sugar in a large bowl. In a separate bowl, mix together the soya yogurt, egg replacement, melted vegan butter, sunflower oil and vanilla extract. Add to the flour mixture and mix together with a fork until only just combined. Fold in the berries.

Divide the mixture between the muffin cases. Bake in a preheated oven, 200°C (400°F), Gas Mark 6, for 15 minutes or until the muffins are well risen and the tops are cracked and golden brown. Leave to cool in the tin for 5 minutes, then transfer to a wire rack. Serve warm or cold.

For 7 g more protein per muffin, add 125 g (4 oz) vanilla vegan protein powder. If the muffin mixture is too thick, add 2 tablespoons soya or other plant-based milk.

For High-protein Double Chocolate Chip Muffins

Make the muffin mixture as above, mixing 125 g (4 oz) vegan chocolate protein powder with the other dry ingredients and swapping the berries for 85 g (3¼ oz) vegan chocolate chips. Add 2 tablespoons soya or other plant-based milk if the mixture is too thick. Bake as above.

Power Bars

50 MINUTES					
16 SERVINGS	282	KCAL / BAR	3 G	FIBRE	
	7 G	PROTEIN	14 G	SUGAR	
	18 G	FAT	7 G	SAT FAT	
	25 G	CARBS	14 MG	SODIUM	

200 g (7 oz) vegan butter

150 g (5 oz) light muscovado sugar

4 tablespoons golden syrup

100 g (3½ oz) mixed seeds, such as sesame, sunflower, pumpkin, hemp and flaxseeds

50 g (2 oz) whole unblanched almonds

50 g (2 oz) hazelnuts

1 dessert apple, cored and diced but not peeled

1 small banana, roughly mashed

200 g (7 oz) porridge oats

60 g (2¼ oz) vegan protein powder

50 ml (2 fl oz) plant-based milk

Line an 18 x 28 cm (7 x 11 inch) roasting tin with nonstick baking paper.

Put the vegan butter, sugar and golden syrup in a large saucepan and heat gently until melted, stirring occasionally. Remove the pan from the heat and stir in all the remaining ingredients. Transfer the mixture to the lined tin and press into an even layer.

Bake in a preheated oven, 180°C (350°F), Gas Mark 4, for 25–30 minutes until golden brown and just beginning to darken around the edges. Leave to cool for 10 minutes, then mark into 16 bars and leave to cool completely in the tin.

Lift out of the tin using the lining paper, cut the bars right through and peel off the paper. Store the bars in an airtight container for up to 3 days – these are energy boosters and therefore ideal for adding to lunchboxes.

For Sesame & Banana Flapjacks

Melt the vegan butter, sugar and golden syrup as above, then stir in 50 g (2 oz) sesame seeds instead of the mixed seeds. Omit the nuts and apple and mix in 2 small peeled and mashed bananas, 250 g (8 oz) porridge oats, 60 g (2¼ oz) vegan protein powder and 50 ml (2 fl oz) plant-based milk. Press the mixture into a shallow 20 cm (8 inch) square cake tin lined with nonstick baking paper and bake as above for 25 minutes until golden. Leave to cool, then lift out, cut into 16 small squares and peel off the paper.

Borlotti Bean & Pepper Bruschetta

20
MINUTES

4
SERVINGS

493	KCAL / SERVING	4 G	FIBRE
19 G	PROTEIN	4 G	SUGAR
13 G	FAT	2 G	SAT FAT
75 G	CARBS	1107 MG	SODIUM

1 large baguette, cut into 8 slices

3 tablespoons olive oil

1 garlic clove, peeled

400 g (13 oz) can borlotti beans, rinsed
   and drained

3 spring onions, sliced

100 g (3½ oz) roasted red peppers
   from a jar, drained and finely sliced

6 basil leaves, thinly shredded

salt and pepper

Place the slices of baguette on a baking sheet and drizzle with 2 tablespoons of the olive oil. Cook under a preheated hot grill for 2–3 minutes on each side until toasted and golden.

Rub each slice of toast with the garlic clove.

Put the borlotti beans and spring onions in a bowl and lightly crush together with a fork. Stir in the roasted peppers, basil, remaining olive oil and salt and pepper to taste.

Spoon the bean mixture on to the toasted baguette slices and serve immediately.

Asparagus Frittata

45 MINUTES					
4 SERVINGS	287	KCAL / SERVING	2 G	FIBRE	
	23 G	PROTEIN	3 G	SUGAR	
	15 G	FAT	3 G	SAT FAT	
	15 G	CARBS	699 MG	SODIUM	

400 g (13 oz) asparagus

2 tablespoons olive oil

400 g (13 oz) firm tofu, drained

1 tablespoon cornflour

2 tablespoons nutritional yeast flakes

½ teaspoon onion powder

½ teaspoon garlic powder

¼ teaspoon ground turmeric

2 tablespoons soya milk

½ teaspoon kala namak (black salt)
   (optional)

50 g (2 oz) Parmesan-style vegan
   cheese, grated

salt and pepper

Break the woody ends off the asparagus and discard. Toss the asparagus in 1 tablespoon of the olive oil.

Heat a griddle pan until hot. Add the asparagus and cook for 4–5 minutes, turning frequently, until starting to look a little charred. Cut the spears into thirds.

Add the tofu to a blender or food processor along with the cornflour, nutritional yeast, onion and garlic powders, turmeric, soya milk, kala namak, if using, and some salt and pepper and blend together until smooth. Transfer to a bowl, then mix in the griddled asparagus and vegan cheese.

Heat the remaining oil in an ovenproof frying pan (such as a cast-iron skillet). Pour the mixture into the pan and bake in a preheated oven, 190°C (375°F), Gas Mark 5, for 25–30 minutes until the frittata is set in the middle and slightly golden on top.

Turn the frittata out on to a board, cut into wedges and serve immediately, or chill and serve with salad.

For 10 g more protein per serving, serve with a chickpea salad. To make, mix a rinsed and drained 400 g (13 oz) can chickpeas with ½ red onion, ¼ cucumber and 70 g (2¼ oz) tomatoes, all chopped, plus 30 g (1¼ oz) rocket leaves.

Broad Bean & Pea Crostini

25 MINUTES

6 SERVINGS

395	KCAL / SERVING	10 G	FIBRE
15 G	PROTEIN	7 G	SUGAR
15 G	FAT	3 G	SAT FAT
51 G	CARBS	587 MG	SODIUM

75 ml (3 fl oz) olive oil

3 strips of lemon rind

2 garlic cloves, peeled

300 g (10 oz) fresh or frozen
broad beans

300 g (10 oz) fresh or frozen peas

handful of mint leaves

6 slices of sourdough bread

salt and pepper

TO SERVE

2 radishes, thinly sliced

handful of pea shoots

25 g (1 oz) Parmesan-style vegan
cheese, shaved

Put the olive oil, lemon rind and garlic cloves in a small saucepan and cook over a very low heat for 7–10 minutes. Remove the pan from the heat and discard the lemon rind.

Cook the broad beans and peas in a saucepan of lightly salted boiling water for 3 minutes until just soft. Drain and rinse under cold running water to cool. Peel the broad beans and discard the shells.

Transfer most of the peas and beans to a blender or food processor, add the mint and cooked garlic together with the flavoured oil and pulse to make a coarse purée. Season well with salt and pepper.

Toast the sourdough, halve the slices and arrange on a serving platter. Spread with the purée and scatter with the reserved peas and broad beans. Top with the radishes, pea shoots and Parmesan-style vegan cheese shavings and serve.

Plant-based Mince & Courgette Koftas

40 MINUTES			
4 SERVINGS			

198	KCAL / SERVING	2 G	FIBRE
15 G	PROTEIN	5 G	SUGAR
9 G	FAT	0 G	SAT FAT
17 G	CARBS	337 MG	SODIUM

2 courgettes, finely grated

2 tablespoons sesame seeds

250 g (8 oz) plant-based mince

2 spring onions, finely chopped

1 garlic clove, crushed

1 tablespoon chopped mint

½ teaspoon ground mixed spice

2 tablespoons dried breadcrumbs

45 g (1¾ oz) liquid vegan egg replacement or 1 tablespoon ground flaxseeds mixed with 3 tablespoons hot water

vegetable oil, for shallow-frying

salt and pepper

lemon wedges, to garnish

Put the courgettes in a sieve and press down to extract as much liquid as possible. Transfer to a bowl.

Heat a dry heavy-based frying pan until hot, add the sesame seeds and cook over a medium heat, shaking the pan constantly, for 1–2 minutes until golden brown and aromatic. Add to the courgettes along with all the remaining ingredients, except the oil for shallow-frying and lemon wedges. Season well with salt and pepper.

Form the mixture into 20 small balls. Heat a shallow depth of oil in a frying pan, add the koftas, in batches, and cook for 5 minutes, turning frequently, until evenly browned. Keep the cooked koftas warm in a preheated oven, 160°C (325°F), Gas Mark 3, while you cook the remainder. Serve hot, garnished with lemon wedges.

For Tahini Sauce to serve as an accompaniment

Mix together 250 ml (8 fl oz) Greek-style plant-based yogurt, 2 crushed garlic cloves, 1 tablespoon tahini paste, 2 teaspoons lemon juice and salt and pepper to taste in a bowl.

Cheat's Pepper Pizza

15
MINUTES

4
SERVINGS

396	KCAL / SERVING	2 G	FIBRE
19 G	PROTEIN	6 G	SUGAR
11 G	FAT	0.5 G	SAT FAT
51 G	CARBS	781 MG	SODIUM

200 g (7 oz) plant-based chicken pieces

4 large pitta breads

4 tablespoons tomato ketchup

4 ready-roasted red and yellow
    peppers from a jar, drained
    and sliced

4 spring onions, sliced

150 g (5 oz) mozzarella-style vegan
    cheese, sliced

small handful of rocket leaves

Cook the plant-based chicken pieces according to the
pack instructions until golden and cooked through.

Toast the pitta breads for 2 minutes on each side.
Top each one with 1 tablespoon tomato ketchup and
the roasted peppers, spring onions, mozzarella-style
vegan cheese and plant-based chicken pieces.

Place under a preheated hot grill and cook for
4–6 minutes, until bubbling and golden. Serve
topped with the rocket.

Chickpea, Tomato & Pepper Salad

30 MINUTES				
4 SERVINGS	333	KCAL / SERVING	12 G	FIBRE
	11 G	PROTEIN	16 G	SUGAR
	17 G	FAT	2 G	SAT FAT
	41 G	CARBS	550 MG	SODIUM

3 large red peppers, cored,
    deseeded and cut into quarters

6 plum tomatoes, halved

4 tablespoons olive oil

1 teaspoon cumin seeds

1 tablespoon lemon juice

½ teaspoon Dijon mustard

½ teaspoon maple syrup

400 g (13 oz) can chickpeas, rinsed
    and drained

100 g (3½ oz) baby spinach leaves

10–12 basil leaves, roughly torn

salt and pepper

Place the peppers and tomatoes in a roasting tin and toss with 1 tablespoon of the olive oil and the cumin seeds. Season with salt and pepper and roast in a preheated oven, 220°C (425°F), Gas Mark 7, for 20 minutes.

Whisk the remaining oil with the lemon juice, mustard and maple syrup in a bowl to make a dressing.

Remove the roasted peppers and tomatoes from the oven and spoon into a salad bowl. Toss in the chickpeas, spinach and basil, pour over the dressing and serve immediately.

Griddled Greek-style Sandwiches

20 MINUTES			
2 SERVINGS			

400	KCAL / SERVING	6 G	FIBRE
7 G	PROTEIN	5 G	SUGAR
22 G	FAT	17 G	SAT FAT
47 G	CARBS	353 MG	SODIUM

¼ small red onion, thinly sliced

8 cherry tomatoes, quartered

4 pitted black olives, chopped

5 cm (2 inch) piece of cucumber, deseeded and cut into small pieces

50 g (2 oz) feta-style vegan cheese, crumbled

1 teaspoon dried oregano

1 teaspoon lemon juice

2 round seeded pitta breads

25 g (1 oz) Cheddar-style vegan cheese, grated

olive oil, for brushing

pepper

Mix together the onion, tomatoes, olives, cucumber, feta-style vegan cheese and oregano in a bowl. Add the lemon juice, season to taste with pepper and gently mix.

Split each pitta bread in half horizontally. Divide the feta-style vegan cheese mixture between the bottom halves of the pitta breads, then add the Cheddar-style vegan cheese. Cover with the top halves of the pitta breads.

Brush a griddle pan with olive oil and heat until hot. Add the sandwiches, press down gently with a spatula and cook for 2–3 minutes on each side until golden and the cheese inside has melted. Serve immediately.

Energizing Lunches

Mediterranean Beans

20 MINUTES	377	KCAL / SERVING	12 G	FIBRE
	20 G	PROTEIN	5 G	SUGAR
4 SERVINGS	17 G	FAT	9 G	SAT FAT
	54 G	CARBS	948 MG	SODIUM

2 tablespoons extra virgin olive oil

1 red onion, diced

1 garlic clove, crushed

½ teaspoon cumin seeds

400 g (13 oz) can cannellini beans, rinsed and drained

75 g (3 oz) cherry tomatoes, quartered

2 teaspoons chopped sage

4 slices of crusty bread

salt and pepper

25 g (1 oz) Parmesan-style vegan cheese, grated, to serve

Heat the olive oil in a large frying pan, add the onion and cook for 1–2 minutes. Add the garlic and cumin seeds and cook for a further 2–3 minutes until the onion is softened and the mixture is aromatic.

Add the beans and mix well to allow them to soak up the flavours, then add the tomatoes. Stir in the sage, season with salt and pepper and heat through.

Meanwhile, toast the bread under a preheated hot grill for 2–3 minutes on each side.

Spoon the beans over the toasted bread, sprinkle with the Parmesan-style vegan cheese and serve.

For Edamame & Pea Soup with Pesto

Prepare the pesto as opposite (or use shop-bought vegan pesto). Heat the olive oil in a saucepan, add the leek and potato as opposite with 1 crushed garlic clove and cook over a gentle heat for 5 minutes until softened. Add the stock as opposite along with 250 g (8 oz) each frozen peas and shelled edamame beans. Bring to the boil, then reduce the heat, cover and simmer for 15 minutes. Stir in 4 tablespoons of the pesto and then blend the soup, in batches, in a blender or food processor until smooth. Reheat and serve as opposite.

Edamame & Pesto Soup

40 MINUTES

4 SERVINGS

660	KCAL / SERVING		9.5 G	FIBRE
21 G	PROTEIN		8 G	SUGARS
47 G	FAT		8 G	SAT FAT
45 G	CARBS		1190 MG	SODIUM

1 tablespoon olive oil

1 leek, trimmed, cleaned and chopped

1 medium-sized potato, peeled
and chopped

575 ml (18 fl oz) vegan vegetable stock

500 g (1 lb) frozen shelled
edamame beans

salt and pepper

100 g (3½ oz) ciabatta bread
croutons, to serve

PESTO

50 g (2 oz) pine nuts, toasted

2 large handfuls of basil, plus extra
leaves to garnish

1 garlic clove, peeled

50 g (2 oz) Parmesan-style
vegan cheese

100 ml (3½ fl oz) olive oil

For the pesto, pulse the pine nuts, basil, garlic and Parmesan-style vegan cheese in a food processor until finely chopped. With the motor running, gradually add the olive oil until blended. Season with salt and pepper and set aside.

Heat the olive oil in a saucepan, add the leek and potato and cook over a gentle heat for 5 minutes until softened. Add the stock and bring to the boil, then reduce the heat, cover and simmer for 10 minutes.

Stir in the edamame beans and cook for a further 5 minutes, then stir in 4 tablespoons of the pesto.

Transfer the soup, in batches, to the food processor or a blender and blend until smooth. Return to the pan and reheat, then season with salt and pepper and add more pesto, if liked, to taste (any extra to requirements will keep in an airtight container in the refrigerator for several days).

Ladle the soup into bowls, then spoon over a little more pesto, if liked, garnish with basil leaves and serve with ciabatta croutons.

For 2 g more protein per serving, instead of using vegan cheese in the pesto add 2 tablespoons nutritional yeast flakes, and swap the ciabatta croutons for toasted wholemeal bread.

Chunky Tomato & Bean Stew

40			
MINUTES			

611	KCAL / SERVING	25 G	FIBRE
26 G	PROTEIN	18 G	SUGAR
17 G	FAT	4 G	SAT FAT
93 G	CARBS	1765 MG	SODIUM

4
SERVINGS

2 tablespoons olive oil

1 red onion, chopped

1 carrot, peeled and cut into chunks

2 garlic cloves, crushed

1 courgette, cut into chunks

1 red chilli, deseeded and chopped

2 teaspoons chopped thyme leaves

2 teaspoons smoked paprika

2 x 400 g (13 oz) cans chickpeas,
  rinsed and drained

425 g (15 oz) can mixed beans in
  chilli sauce

400 g (13 oz) can chopped tomatoes

150 ml (¼ pint) vegan vegetable stock

4 small corn tortillas

salt and pepper

Heat the olive oil in a saucepan, add the onion and carrot and cook over a gentle heat for 5 minutes until softened. Stir in the garlic, courgette, chilli, thyme and smoked paprika and cook for a further 5 minutes.

Stir the chickpeas, the beans with their sauce, tomatoes and stock into the pan. Bring to the boil, then reduce the heat and simmer for 10 minutes until the vegetables are tender and the stew has thickened slightly.

Meanwhile, cut the corn tortillas into triangles, spread out on a baking sheet in a single layer and bake in a preheated oven, 190°C (375°F), Gas Mark 5 for about 10 minutes until crisp.

Season the stew with salt and pepper and serve hot with the homemade corn tortilla chips.

Creamy Vegan Tuna & Leek Pasta

25 MINUTES		
2 SERVINGS		

666	KCAL / SERVING	1 G	FIBRE
24 G	PROTEIN	13 G	SUGAR
21 G	FAT	4 G	SAT FAT
94 G	CARBS	318 MG	SODIUM

400 g (13 oz) dried penne

2 tablespoons extra virgin olive oil

2 leeks, trimmed, cleaned and sliced

2 large garlic cloves, sliced

300 g (10 oz) plant-based tuna

150 ml (¼ pint) vegan dry white wine

150 ml (¼ pint) plant-based
     single cream

2 tablespoons chopped flat
     leaf parsley

salt and pepper

rocket salad, to serve (optional)

Cook the pasta in a large saucepan of lightly salted boiling water for 10–12 minutes or according to the pack instructions until al dente. Drain well and return to the pan.

Meanwhile, heat the olive oil in a frying pan, add the leeks, garlic and salt and pepper to taste and cook gently for 5 minutes until the leeks are softened.

Add the plant-based tuna and cook, stirring, for 1 minute. Add the wine, bring to the boil and boil until reduced by half. Stir in the plant-based cream and heat through for 2–3 minutes.

Add the plant-based tuna sauce to the drained pasta with the parsley and stir over a medium heat for 1 minute. Serve immediately with a rocket salad, if liked.

For Vegan Chicken, Leek & Rocket Pasta

While the pasta is cooking as above, heat 4 tablespoons extra virgin olive oil in a frying pan, add 2 trimmed, cleaned and sliced leeks, 2 crushed garlic cloves and 2 deseeded and sliced red chillies and cook gently for 5 minutes. Add 250 g (8 oz) diced plant-based chicken pieces and cook over a medium-high heat, turning frequently, for about 5 minutes or until golden and cooked through. Stir into the cooked, drained pasta with 150 g (5 oz) rocket leaves, a squeeze of lemon juice and a little extra oil. Serve immediately.

Marinated Tofu with Vegetables

30 MINUTES, PLUS MARINATING

4 SERVINGS

380	KCAL / SERVING	3 G	FIBRE
30 G	PROTEIN	15 G	SUGAR
18 G	FAT	3 G	SAT FAT
25 G	CARBS	1869 MG	SODIUM

3 tablespoons kecap manis or sweet soy sauce

1 teaspoon crushed garlic

2 teaspoons very finely chopped fresh root ginger

2 tablespoons sweet chilli dipping sauce

500 g (1 lb) firm tofu, drained and cut into 1.5 cm (¾ inch) slices

2 tablespoons vegetable or groundnut oil

1 carrot, peeled and cut into fine matchsticks

500 g (1 lb) pak choi, sliced

225 g (7½ oz) can bamboo shoots in water, rinsed and drained

200 g (7 oz) bean sprouts

6 tablespoons vegan oyster sauce

2 teaspoons sesame seeds, to garnish

Mix together the kecap manis or sweet soy sauce, garlic, ginger and sweet chilli dipping sauce in a small bowl. Arrange the tofu slices in a shallow dish and pour over the marinade, turning to coat. Set aside to marinate for about 20 minutes.

Transfer the tofu slices to a foil-lined grill rack, reserving the marinade. Cook under a preheated hot grill for about 3 minutes on each side until golden. Remove from the heat and keep warm.

Meanwhile, heat the oil in a wok over a medium heat. Add the carrot and pak choi and stir-fry for 4–5 minutes until beginning to soften. Add the bamboo shoots and bean sprouts and stir-fry for 1 minute. Pour in the reserved tofu marinade and vegan oyster sauce and heat until bubbling.

Spoon the stir-fried vegetables into deep bowls, top with the grilled tofu slices and sprinkle with the sesame seeds.

For High-protein Tofu & Vegetable Noodles

Cook the stir-fried vegetables as above, adding 160 g (5½ oz) ready-prepared marinated tofu strips or cubed firm tofu along with the bamboo shoots and bean sprouts. Meanwhile, cook 200 g (7 oz) dried black bean noodles according to the pack instructions, then drain and toss with the vegetables and tofu. Serve with soy sauce, to taste.

Lentil, Mustard & Chickpea Soup

40 MINUTES

4 SERVINGS

256	KCAL / SERVING	10 G	FIBRE
14 G	PROTEIN	7 G	SUGAR
4 G	FAT	0 G	SAT FAT
45 G	CARBS	997 MG	SODIUM

½ teaspoon coconut or olive oil

¼ teaspoon mustard seeds

½ teaspoon ground cumin

½ teaspoon ground turmeric

1 small onion, diced

1.5 cm (¾ inch) piece of fresh root
ginger, finely chopped

1 garlic clove, finely chopped

100 g (3½ oz) dried red split lentils,
rinsed and drained

400 g (13 oz) can chickpeas, rinsed
and drained

900 ml (1½ pints) hot vegan
vegetable stock

50 g (2 oz) baby spinach leaves

salt and pepper

Heat the oil in a saucepan and add the dry spices. When the mustard seeds start to pop, add the onion, ginger and garlic and cook for a few minutes until the onion is softened. Add the lentils and chickpeas and stir well to coat.

Pour in the stock and bring to the boil, then reduce the heat and simmer for about 15 minutes until the lentils are tender.

Stir in the spinach and cook until wilted, then season to taste with salt and pepper. Ladle the soup into bowls and serve immediately.

For 6 g more protein, add 1 slice of wholemeal toast to each serving.

For No-cook Lentil & Chickpea Salad

Chop 150 g (5 oz) cherry tomatoes, 1 red onion and a handful of fresh coriander and add to a large serving bowl. Add a rinsed and drained 400 g (13 oz can) each of chickpeas and brown lentils along with the finely grated zest of 1 lemon. For the dressing, put the juice of ½ lemon, 1 teaspoon olive oil, 1 teaspoon Dijon mustard, ¼ teaspoon ground cumin and a pinch of salt in a small container with a lid. Seal with the lid and thoroughly shake to combine the ingredients. Toss the salad with the dressing and 100 g (3½ oz) crumbled feta-style vegan cheese.

Chilli & Courgette Penne

25 MINUTES	501	KCAL / SERVING	2 G	FIBRE
	22 G	PROTEIN	4 G	SUGAR
4 SERVINGS	20 G	FAT	11 G	SAT FAT
	55 G	CARBS	300 MG	SODIUM

15 g (½ oz) vegan butter

1 tablespoon olive oil

4 spring onions, very finely chopped

3 courgettes, coarsely grated

2 red chillies, finely chopped

2 garlic cloves, finely chopped

finely grated zest of 1 lime

150 g (5 oz) vegan cream cheese

350 g (11½ oz) dried chickpea
   penne or other short chickpea
   pasta shapes

small handful of flat leaf
   parsley, chopped

salt and pepper

Melt the vegan butter with the olive oil in a large frying pan, add the spring onions, courgettes, chillies and garlic and cook over a medium-low heat for 10 minutes or until the vegetables are softened.

Reduce the heat to low, add the lime zest and gently cook for 3–4 minutes, then add the vegan cream cheese and mix together until the cheese melts. Season to taste with salt and pepper.

Meanwhile, cook the pasta in a large saucepan of lightly salted boiling water for 6–9 minutes or according to the pack instructions until al dente.

Drain the pasta, then stir into the courgette mixture with the parsley. Spoon into warm bowls and serve immediately.

For Creamy Plant-based Chicken & Bacon Pasta

Cook the spring onions and garlic only in the vegan butter and olive oil until softened as above, then stir in the vegan cream cheese until melted. Set aside. Heat 1 tablespoon olive oil in a frying pan and cook 120 g (4 oz) diced plant-based bacon and 200 g (7 oz) diced plant-based chicken pieces over a medium-high heat, turning frequently, for about 5 minutes until the plant-based bacon is crisp and the plant-based chicken is golden and cooked through. Add to the creamy sauce with cooked pasta of your choice. Spoon into warm bowls and serve sprinkled with the chopped flat leaf parsley as above.

For Spicy Bean Enchiladas

Pan-fry 150 g (5 oz) plant-based mince according to the pack instructions. Spread the refried beans as opposite over all 8 soft flour tortillas. Top each tortilla with a couple of spoonfuls of the plant-based mince, the jalapeños as opposite, 2 large diced tomatoes, 1 cored, deseeded and finely chopped red pepper and 2 sliced spring onions. Tuck in the ends and roll each tortilla up tightly, then place in an ovenproof dish to fit snugly. Pour a 300 g (10 oz) jar hot Mexican salsa over the tortillas, then dot with small spoonfuls of the soured soya yogurt and sprinkle with the grated Cheddar-style vegan cheese as opposite. Cook in a preheated oven, 220°C (425°F), Gas Mark 7, for 20–25 minutes until hot and bubbling. Serve hot with shredded iceberg lettuce and 1 tablespoon finely chopped fresh coriander, if liked.

Quick Quesadillas

30 MINUTES	590	KCAL / SERVING	8 G	FIBRE
	23 G	PROTEIN	6 G	SUGAR
4 SERVINGS	18 G	FAT	10 G	SAT FAT
	88 G	CARBS	1030 MG	SODIUM

150 g (5 oz) plant-based chicken pieces

200 g (7 oz) refried beans

8 soft flour tortillas

25 g (1 oz) sliced jalapeños from a jar, drained and chopped

1 large tomato, deseeded and diced

100 g (3½ oz) Cheddar-style vegan cheese, grated

2 spring onions, sliced

1 tablespoon finely chopped fresh coriander (optional)

100 ml (3½ fl oz) unsweetened natural soya yogurt soured with a squeeze of lemon juice, to serve (optional)

Cook the plant-based chicken pieces according to the pack instructions until golden and cooked through. Chop into small pieces.

Spread the refried beans over 4 of the tortillas. Top with the plant-based chicken, jalapeños, tomato, vegan cheese, spring onions and coriander, if using. Cover each one with another tortilla to make 4 quesadillas.

Heat a large griddle pan until hot. Griddle the quesadillas, one at a time, over a medium-high heat for about 30–60 seconds on each side until lightly browned and the cheese inside has melted.

Cut the quesadillas into quarters and serve immediately, with the soured soya yogurt, if liked.

For 25 g more protein per serving, swap the regular flour tortillas for wholemeal tortillas.

For Puy Lentil & Sun-dried Tomato Salad

Put 200 g (7 oz) rinsed and drained dried Puy lentils in a saucepan, cover generously with cold water and bring to the boil. Reduce the heat and simmer for 15 minutes until just tender. Drain and transfer to a bowl. Toss with the juice of 1 lemon, 1 crushed garlic clove and 4 tablespoons olive oil, then season with salt and pepper. Stir a drained 280 g (9¼ oz) jar sun-dried tomatoes, 1 small finely chopped red onion and a handful of chopped flat leaf parsley through the lentils and serve with 60 g (2¼ oz) rocket leaves and 100 g (3½ oz) bread croutons.

Puy Lentil Stew with Garlic Bread

45 MINUTES			
4 SERVINGS			

629	KCAL / SERVING	12 G	FIBRE
21 G	PROTEIN	8 G	SUGAR
24 G	FAT	28 G	SAT FAT
72 G	CARBS	675 MG	SODIUM

4 tablespoons olive oil

1 red pepper, cored, deseeded and cut into chunks

1 green pepper, cored, deseeded and cut into chunks

1 red onion, roughly chopped

1 garlic clove, sliced

1 fennel bulb, trimmed and sliced

250 g (8 oz) dried Puy lentils, rinsed and drained

600 ml (1 pint) vegan vegetable stock

300 ml (½ pint) vegan red wine

50 g (2 oz) vegan butter, softened

1 garlic clove, crushed

2 tablespoons thyme leaves, roughly chopped

1 wholemeal French baguette

salt and pepper

Heat the olive oil in a large, heavy-based saucepan, add the peppers, onion, garlic and fennel and cook over a medium-high heat, stirring frequently, for 5 minutes until softened and lightly browned. Stir in the lentils, stock and wine and bring to the boil, then reduce the heat and simmer for 25 minutes until the lentils are tender.

Meanwhile, beat the vegan butter with the garlic and thyme in a small bowl and season with a little salt and pepper. Cut the baguette into thick slices, almost all the way through but leaving the base attached. Spread the butter thickly over each slice, then wrap the baguette in foil and place in a preheated oven, 200°C (400°F), Gas Mark 6, for 15 minutes.

Serve the stew hot, ladled into warm serving bowls, with the torn hot garlic and herb bread on the side for mopping up the juices.

↑

For 5 g extra protein, add 1 tablespoon unsweetened natural soya yogurt and 1 tablespoon hulled hemp seeds to each serving.

Tikka Lentil Koftas

40 MINUTES					
4 SERVINGS	493	KCAL / SERVING	19 G	FIBRE	
	25 G	PROTEIN	11 G	SUGAR	
	16 G	FAT	1 G	SAT FAT	
	66 G	CARBS	601 MG	SODIUM	

3 tablespoons sunflower oil

1 onion, finely chopped

1 garlic clove, crushed

1 teaspoon peeled and chopped
    fresh root ginger

1 green chilli, deseeded and
    finely chopped

2 tablespoons tikka curry paste

finely grated zest and juice of ½ lemon

2 x 400 g (13 oz) cans green lentils,
    rinsed and drained

2 tablespoons chopped
    fresh coriander

25 g (1 oz) fresh white breadcrumbs

plain flour, for coating

45 g (1¾ oz) liquid vegan egg
    replacement or 1 tablespoon
    ground flaxseeds mixed with
    3 tablespoons hot water

75 g (3 oz) dried breadcrumbs

salt and pepper

green salad leaves, to serve (optional)

Heat 1 tablespoon of the sunflower oil in a large saucepan, add the onion, garlic, ginger and chilli and cook over a medium heat for 3–4 minutes until softened. Stir in the curry paste and lemon zest and juice and cook, stirring, for 1 minute.

Remove the pan from the heat and stir in the lentils, coriander and fresh breadcrumbs, then season well with salt and pepper. Mix well, mashing with a spoon so that the mixture holds together.

Divide the mixture into 8 equal portions, using slightly wet hands. Flatten slightly, then roll in flour to coat. Place the egg replacement and dried breadcrumbs in separate dishes. Dip each kofta in the egg replacement and then in the dried breadcrumbs until coated.

Heat the remaining oil in a large saucepan, add the koftas and fry over a medium heat for 4–5 minutes on each side until crisp and golden. Serve with green salad leaves, if liked.

For 4 g more protein per serving, serve the koftas with a cucumber and mint soya yogurt raita. To make, mix together 225 ml (7½ fl oz) natural soya yogurt, ¼ grated cucumber, 2 tablespoons chopped mint, the juice of ¼ lemon and a pinch of salt in a small bowl.

Spicy Edamame Bean & Noodle Salad

20 MINUTES		
4 SERVINGS		

366	KCAL / SERVING	4 G	FIBRE
17 G	PROTEIN	10 G	SUGAR
9 G	FAT	1 G	SAT FAT
59 G	CARBS	1374 MG	SODIUM

250 g (8 oz) dried soba noodles

250 g (8 oz) frozen shelled
   edamame beans

6 spring onions, thinly sliced diagonally

2 tablespoons sesame seeds

salt

chopped fresh coriander leaves,
   to garnish

DRESSING

3 cm (1¼ inch) piece of fresh root
   ginger, peeled and grated

1 red chilli, finely chopped

3 tablespoons mirin

3 tablespoons light soy sauce

1 tablespoon toasted sesame oil

1 teaspoon maple syrup

Cook the noodles and edamame beans in a saucepan of lightly salted boiling water for 4–5 minutes or according to the noodle pack instructions. Drain well, then return to the pan and add the spring onions. Cover and keep warm.

Heat a dry heavy-based frying pan until hot, add the sesame seeds and cook over a medium heat, shaking the pan constantly, for 1–2 minutes until golden brown and aromatic. Remove from the pan and set aside.

Mix together all the dressing ingredients in a bowl. Pour over the noodle mixture and toss to mix well.

Ladle the noodle mixture into warm bowls, then scatter over the toasted sesame seeds, garnish with chopped coriander and serve.

For 10 g more protein, add 50 g (2 oz) pan-fried tempeh cubes per serving. Heat a splash of sunflower oil in a frying pan and cook the tempeh cubes over a medium-high heat, turning frequently, for about 10 minutes until browned on all sides.

Flatbread, Roasted Veg & Hummus

50					
MINUTES, PLUS STANDING	426	KCAL / SERVING	13 G	FIBRE	
	15 G	PROTEIN	10 G	SUGAR	
4	12 G	FAT	2 G	SAT FAT	
SERVINGS	70 G	CARBS	607 MG	SODIUM	

200 g (7 oz) wholemeal plain flour, plus extra for dusting

½ teaspoon salt

1 red pepper, cored, deseeded and cut into chunks

1 orange pepper, cored, deseeded and cut into chunks

1 green pepper, cored, deseeded and cut into chunks

1 large red onion, cut into thin wedges

2 tablespoons olive oil

½ teaspoon ground coriander

½ teaspoon cumin seeds

HUMMUS

400 g (13 oz) can chickpeas, drained well, reserving 3 tablespoons liquid from the can (aquafaba)

finely grated zest and juice of 1 lemon

3 tablespoons chopped flat leaf parsley

1 tablespoon tahini

salt and pepper

Mix the flour and salt together in a bowl, then add enough water to bring the mixture together into a dough – about 7–8 tablespoons. Turn out on to a lightly floured surface and knead well until smooth. Return to the bowl, cover with clingfilm and leave in a warm place for 30 minutes.

Toss the peppers and onion with the olive oil in a large roasting tin, then add the coriander and cumin and toss again. Roast in a preheated oven, 220°C (425°F), Gas Mark 7, for 20 minutes until softened.

Meanwhile, blend together all the hummus ingredients in a blender or food processor until smooth.

Divide the flatbread dough into 4 pieces and roll out each on a lightly floured surface into a 25 cm (10 inch) round. Heat a large frying pan until hot and cook the flatbreads, one at a time, for about 45 seconds on each side until lightly golden, flipping over with a spatula.

Spread each warm flatbread with some of the hummus, then top with one-quarter of the hot roasted vegetables and fold over to serve.

Tofu with Pak Choi & Spring Onions

40 MINUTES	342	KCAL / SERVING	3 G	FIBRE
4 SERVINGS	23 G	PROTEIN	7 G	SUGAR
	21 G	FAT	7 G	SAT FAT
	18 G	CARBS	758 MG	SODIUM

2 tablespoons sunflower oil

8 garlic cloves, roughly chopped

4 shallots, finely chopped

2 red chillies, sliced

7 cm (3 inch) length of trimmed lemon
  grass stalk, finely chopped

2 teaspoons peeled and grated fresh
  root ginger

1 teaspoon ground turmeric

400 ml (14 fl oz) can light coconut milk

200 ml (7 fl oz) hot vegan
  vegetable stock

400 g (13 oz) baby pak choi, halved
  or quartered

200 g (7 oz) mangetout

400 g (13 oz) firm tofu, drained
  and cubed

1 tablespoon soy sauce

1 tablespoon lime juice

6 spring onions, thinly sliced

salt and pepper

TO GARNISH

small handful of Thai basil leaves

2 red chillies, sliced

Put the sunflower oil, garlic, shallots, chillies, lemon grass, ginger, turmeric and half the coconut milk in a blender or food processor and blend until fairly smooth.

Heat a large nonstick wok or frying pan until hot, add the coconut milk mixture and stir-fry over a high heat for 3–4 minutes. Add the remaining coconut milk and the stock and bring to the boil, then reduce the heat to low and simmer gently, uncovered, for 6–8 minutes.

Add the pak choi, mangetout and tofu and simmer for a further 6–7 minutes. Stir in the soy sauce and lime juice, then season to taste with salt and pepper and simmer for another 1–2 minutes.

Remove the pan from the heat and stir in the spring onions. Ladle into warm bowls and serve scattered with the Thai basil leaves and sliced red chillies.

↑

For 22 g more protein per serving, serve with 200 g (7 oz) (uncooked weight) dried black bean noodles, cooked according to the pack instructions and divided between the 4 bowls.

Puy Lentil &
Butter Bean Salad

404	KCAL / SERVING	14 G	FIBRE
15 G	PROTEIN	6 G	SUGAR
20 G	FAT	3 G	SAT FAT
43 G	CARBS	365 MG	SODIUM

400 g (13 oz) can Puy lentils, rinsed
and drained

400 g (13 oz) can butter beans, rinsed
and drained

1 red onion, finely sliced

200 g (7 oz) cherry tomatoes, halved

50 g (2 oz) flat leaf parsley,
roughly chopped

DRESSING

6 tablespoons extra virgin olive oil

2 red chillies, very finely diced

2 tablespoons vegan red wine vinegar

1 teaspoon Dijon or wholegrain mustard

1 teaspoon maple syrup

½ garlic clove, crushed

Put the lentils and butter beans in a large serving bowl, then add the onion, cherry tomatoes and parsley.

Mix together all the dressing ingredients in a bowl, then pour over the salad, toss to mix well and serve.

*For 10 g more protein,
add 100 g (3½ oz)
ciabatta bread per serving.*

Delicious Dinners

Chilli Tacos

40 MINUTES	679	KCAL / SERVING	13 G	FIBRE
	35 G	PROTEIN	10 G	SUGAR
4 SERVINGS	21 G	FAT	10 G	SAT FAT
	86 G	CARBS	387 MG	SODIUM

2 tablespoons olive oil

1 large onion, finely chopped

2 garlic cloves, crushed

500 g (1 lb) plant-based mince

700 g (1 lb 7 oz) jar passata

400 g (13 oz) can red kidney beans, rinsed and drained

2 tablespoons hot chilli sauce

8 soft corn tortillas

125 g (4 oz) Cheddar-style vegan cheese, grated

125 ml (4 fl oz) unsweetened natural soya yogurt soured with a squeeze of lemon juice

handful of fresh coriander sprigs

salt and pepper

Heat the olive oil in a saucepan, add the onion and garlic and cook over a medium heat for 5 minutes until softened.

Crumble the plant-based mince into the pan and cook over a medium-high heat, breaking it up with a wooden spoon and stirring frequently, for about 10 minutes until browned. Stir in the passata, beans, chilli sauce and salt and pepper to taste and bring to the boil. Reduce the heat and simmer, uncovered, for 15 minutes until thickened.

Meanwhile, place the corn tortillas on a large baking sheet and heat in a preheated oven, 180°C (350°F), Gas Mark 4, for 5 minutes.

Serve the tortillas on a platter in the centre of the table. Take 2 tortillas per person and spoon some chilli into each one. Top with a quarter of the vegan cheese and soured soya yogurt and a few coriander sprigs, roll up and serve.

For Lentil, Tofu & Red Pepper Chilli

Heat 2 tablespoons olive oil in a saucepan, add 1 finely chopped large onion and 200 g (7 oz) drained, patted dry and crumbled firm tofu and cook, stirring, until the tofu is starting to brown. Then add 1 large cored, deseeded and chopped red pepper and 2 crushed garlic cloves and cook over a high heat for 5 minutes. Add 2 x 400 g (13 oz) cans brown lentils, rinsed and drained, together with the passata, red kidney beans, chilli sauce and salt and pepper to taste as opposite. Bring to the boil, then reduce the heat and simmer, uncovered, for 15 minutes. Meanwhile, cook 300 g (10 oz) basmati rice in a large saucepan of salted boiling water for 10–12 minutes until just tender, then drain. Serve the chilli hot with the rice, 150 g (5 oz) ready-made guacamole and the soured soya yogurt as opposite.

Coconut Dahl with Toasted Naan Fingers

15 MINUTES					
4 SERVINGS	658	KCAL / SERVING	9 G	FIBRE	
	23 G	PROTEIN	5 G	SUGAR	
	32 G	FAT	20 G	SAT FAT	
	78 G	CARBS	611 MG	SODIUM	

1 tablespoon vegetable oil

1 onion, roughly chopped

2 tablespoons korma curry paste

250 g (8 oz) dried red split lentils, rinsed and drained

400 ml (14 fl oz) can coconut milk

240 ml (7¾ fl oz) vegan vegetable stock

handful of fresh coriander leaves, chopped

2 naans

pepper

Heat the vegetable oil in a heavy-based saucepan, add the onion and cook over a high heat, stirring, for 1 minute, then stir in the curry paste and lentils.

Pour in the coconut milk, then fill the can with water and add to the pan along with the vegan vegetable stock. Simmer briskly, uncovered, for 8–9 minutes until the lentils are tender and the mixture is thick and pulpy. Season with pepper and sprinkle over the chopped coriander.

Meanwhile, lightly toast the naans under a preheated hot grill until warm and golden.

Cut the toasted naan into fingers and serve alongside the dahl for dipping.

For Chunky Chickpea & Lentil Dahl

Heat 4 tablespoons vegetable oil in a large saucepan and cook 1 roughly chopped onion over a medium-high heat, stirring occasionally, for 10 minutes until tender. Stir in 4 tablespoons korma curry paste and 125 g (4 oz) dried red split lentils and a 400 g (13 oz) can chickpeas, both rinsed and drained, then pour in 600 ml (1 pint) vegan vegetable stock and simmer, uncovered, for 8–9 minutes until the lentils are tender and the mixture is thick and pulpy. Meanwhile, prepare the toasted naan fingers as above and serve with the dahl.

Lentil Bolognese

40 MINUTES				
4 SERVINGS	600	KCAL / SERVING	21 G	FIBRE
	27 G	PROTEIN	14 G	SUGAR
	15 G	FAT	3 G	SAT FAT
	88 G	CARBS	1098 MG	SODIUM

1 onion, roughly chopped

1 carrot, peeled and chopped

1 celery stick, roughly chopped

1 garlic clove, peeled

3 tablespoons olive oil

125 ml (4 fl oz) vegan red wine

100 ml (3½ fl oz) water

75 g (3 oz) tomato purée

400 g (13 oz) can chopped tomatoes

1 teaspoon dried mixed herbs

2 x 400 g (13 oz) cans green lentils,
    rinsed and drained

50 g (2 oz) Parmesan-style vegan
    cheese, grated

salt and pepper

4 slices of crusty bread, to serve

Put the onion, carrot, celery and garlic in a food processor and pulse briefly until finely chopped.

Heat the olive oil in a large, heavy-based flameproof casserole or saucepan. Add the vegetable mixture and cook, stirring frequently, for 5–6 minutes until softened and lightly golden.

Stir in the wine, measured water, tomato purée, tomatoes and herbs, and season to taste with salt and pepper. Simmer gently, uncovered, for about 15 minutes. Add the lentils and simmer for a further 5–7 minutes until the mixture is thickened and tender.

Spoon into deep bowls, sprinkle with the vegan cheese and serve with the crusty bread.

For 4 g extra protein per serving, swap the white bread for wholemeal bread.

Delicatessen Pasta

20 MINUTES	536	KCAL / SERVING	6 G	FIBRE
4 SERVINGS	25 G	PROTEIN	5 G	SUGAR
	15 G	FAT	4 G	SAT FAT
	75 G	CARBS	73 MG	SODIUM

375 g (12 oz) dried chickpea fusilli

2 tablespoons extra virgin olive oil

1 tablespoon balsamic vinegar

½ teaspoon Dijon mustard

½ teaspoon maple syrup

1 garlic clove, crushed

10 sun-dried tomatoes in oil, drained
and sliced

400 g (13 oz) can artichoke hearts,
drained and halved

100 g (3½ oz) Parmesan-style vegan
cheese, shaved

salt

Cook the pasta in a large saucepan of lightly salted boiling water for 6–9 minutes or according to the pack instructions until al dente.

Meanwhile, whisk together the olive oil, vinegar, mustard, maple syrup and garlic in a small bowl for the dressing.

Drain the pasta and return to the pan with the dressing. Add the sun-dried tomatoes and artichoke hearts and stir to warm through.

Serve in warm shallow pasta bowls, sprinkled with the vegan cheese shavings.

For an extra 8 g protein per serving, steam 600 g (1¼ lb) broccoli and divide between the 4 bowls, then sprinkle each serving with 1 tablespoon hulled hemp seeds.

Chilli Sin Carne

1 HOUR	557	KCAL / SERVING	15 G	FIBRE	
2 SERVINGS	38 G	PROTEIN	19 G	SUGAR	
	18 G	FAT	2 G	SAT FAT	
	66 G	CARBS	2630 MG	SODIUM	

2 tablespoons olive oil

1 red onion, finely chopped

3 garlic cloves, finely chopped

250 g (8 oz) plant-based mince

½ teaspoon ground cumin

1 small red pepper, cored, deseeded
   and diced

400 g (13 oz) can chopped tomatoes

1 tablespoon tomato purée

2 teaspoons chilli powder

1 teaspoon yeast extract

200 ml (7 fl oz) vegan vegetable stock

400 g (13 oz) can red kidney beans,
   rinsed and drained

salt and pepper

TO SERVE (OPTIONAL)

unsweetened natural soya
   yogurt soured with a squeeze
   of lemon juice

spring onions, sliced

90 g (3¼ oz) brown rice, cooked

Heat the olive oil in a saucepan, add the onion and garlic and cook for 5 minutes or until softened.

Crumble in the plant-based mince and add the cumin, then cook over a medium-high heat, breaking it up with a wooden spoon and stirring frequently, for 5–6 minutes until browned.

Stir in the red pepper, tomatoes, tomato purée, chilli powder, yeast extract and stock and bring to the boil. Reduce the heat and simmer gently for 30 minutes.

Add the red kidney beans and cook for a further 5 minutes. Season to taste with salt and pepper. If liked, top with soured yogurt and sliced spring onions and serve with brown rice, cooked according to the pack instructions.

For Chilli Beans with Jackfruit

Soften the onion with the garlic in the olive oil as above, then add a drained 400 g (13 oz) can jackfruit instead of the plant-based mince and cook with the cumin as above. Add the red pepper, tomatoes, tomato purée, chilli powder, yeast extract and stock and cook as above, then stir in a rinsed and drained 400 g (13 oz) can cannellini beans along with the red kidney beans and cook for a final 5 minutes. Season to taste and serve with 90 g (3¼ oz) rinsed and drained quinoa, cooked according to the pack instructions.

For Spicy Chickpea & Tofu Curry with Quinoa

Heat a splash of sunflower oil in a frying pan and cook 200 g (7 oz) drained, patted dry and cubed firm tofu over a medium-high heat, turning frequently, for about 10 minutes until browned on all sides. Omitting the lentils, prepare the chickpea curry as opposite, adding the pan-fried tofu with the chickpeas. Meanwhile, cook 180 g (6 oz) rinsed and drained quinoa according to the pack instructions. Serve the curry drizzled with the whisked soya yogurt, garnished with chopped fresh coriander and along with lemon wedges for squeezing over as opposite, plus 1 chopped red chilli if liked.

Spicy Chickpea Curry

45 MINUTES			
4 SERVINGS			

532	KCAL / SERVING	20 G	FIBRE
26 G	PROTEIN	12 G	SUGAR
14 G	FAT	1 G	SAT FAT
81 G	CARBS	459 MG	SODIUM

150 g (5 oz) dried red split lentils, rinsed and drained

2 tablespoons sunflower oil

4 garlic cloves, crushed

2 teaspoons peeled and finely grated fresh root ginger

1 large onion, coarsely grated

1 green chilli, finely sliced, plus extra to garnish

1 teaspoon hot chilli powder, plus extra to garnish

1 tablespoon ground cumin

1 tablespoon ground coriander

3 tablespoons unsweetened natural soya yogurt, plus extra, whisked, to serve

2 teaspoons garam masala

500 ml (17 fl oz) water

2 teaspoons tamarind paste

2 teaspoons medium or hot curry powder

2 x 400 g (13 oz) cans chickpeas, rinsed and drained

chopped fresh coriander leaves, to garnish

lemon wedges, to serve (optional)

Bring a small saucepan of water to the boil, add the lentils and cook over a medium heat for about 10 minutes until al dente, then drain and set aside.

Meanwhile, heat the sunflower oil in a large, heavy-based frying pan, add the garlic, ginger, onion and green chilli and cook over a medium heat, stirring occasionally, for 5–6 minutes until the onion is lightly golden. Stir in the chilli powder, cumin, ground coriander, yogurt and garam masala and cook for a further 1–2 minutes.

Pour in the measured water and bring to the boil. Stir in the tamarind paste, curry powder, lentils and chickpeas and return to the boil. Reduce the heat to medium and cook, uncovered, for 15–20 minutes or until the mixture is thickened.

Ladle the curry into warm bowls, drizzle with the extra whisked soya yogurt and garnish with chopped coriander, sliced green chillis and hot chilli powder. Serve with lemon wedges for squeezing over, if liked.

For 6 g more of protein per serving, serve with 1 x 60 g (2¼ oz) chapatti, warmed according to the pack instructions, or 45 g (1¾ oz) quinoa, cooked according to the pack instructions.

'Meaty' Boston Beans

2½ HOURS, PLUS SOAKING	431	KCAL / SERVING	3 G	FIBRE
	34 G	PROTEIN	17 G	SUGAR
4 SERVINGS	6 G	FAT	2 G	SAT FAT
	63 G	CARBS	883 MG	SODIUM

300 g (10 oz) dried haricot beans

15 g (½ oz) vegan butter

375 g (12 oz) plant-based mince

1 onion, chopped

1 tablespoon chopped thyme
  or rosemary

400 g (13 oz) can chopped tomatoes

3 tablespoons black treacle

2 tablespoons tomato purée

2 tablespoons wholegrain mustard

1 tablespoon vegan Worcestershire
  sauce or mushroom ketchup

salt and pepper

Soak the dried beans in plenty of cold water overnight.

Drain the beans, put in a flameproof casserole with a lid and cover with cold water. Bring to the boil, then reduce the heat and simmer gently for 15–20 minutes or until the beans have softened slightly. Test by removing a few on a fork and squeezing them gently – they should give a little. Drain the beans.

Wipe out the dish and melt the vegan butter. Crumble in the plant-based mince and cook over a medium-high heat, breaking it up with a wooden spoon and stirring frequently, for about 8 minutes until browned. Add the onion and cook gently for 5 minutes.

Stir in the beans, thyme or rosemary and tomatoes. Add enough water to just cover the ingredients and bring to the boil. Cover with the lid and transfer to a preheated oven, 150°C (300°F), Gas Mark 2. Cook for about 1 hour or until the beans are very tender.

Mix together the treacle, tomato purée, mustard, vegan Worcestershire sauce or mushroom ketchup and salt and pepper to taste in a small bowl. Stir the mixture into the beans, re-cover and return to the oven for a further 30 minutes. Ladle into warm bowls and serve.

For Veggie Bangers & Beans

Soak 300 g (12 oz) dried butter beans overnight, then drain and cook in the same way as the haricot beans opposite. Cook 12 plant-based sausages in the vegan butter in the casserole, turning frequently, for about 8 minutes until lightly browned all over. Remove from the pan and set aside. Add the onion and continue as opposite. Add the plant-based sausages in the final step before the treacle mixture and return to the oven for a further 30 minutes.

For Curried Meat-free Mince Filo Pies

Cook the plant-based mince mixture as opposite, adding 1 tablespoon medium curry paste with the tomatoes, tomato purée and seasoning. Divide the mixture between 6 x 300 ml (½ pint) ovenproof dishes. Layer 4 sheets of filo pastry together, brushing each with melted vegan butter. Cut into 6 and scrunch one over each dish to cover. Bake in a preheated oven, 190°C (375°F), Gas Mark 5, for 20 minutes.

Meat-free Cottage Pie

1¾ HOURS	527	KCAL / SERVING	8 G	FIBRE
4 SERVINGS	27 G	PROTEIN	11 G	SUGAR
	22 G	FAT	11 G	SAT FAT
	58 G	CARBS	780 MG	SODIUM

1 tablespoon olive oil

1 onion, finely chopped

1 carrot, peeled and diced

1 celery stick, diced

1 tablespoon chopped thyme

500 g (1 lb) plant-based mince

400 g (13 oz) can chopped tomatoes

4 tablespoons tomato purée

750 g (1½ lb) potatoes, such as Désirée,
    peeled and cubed

50 g (2 oz) vegan butter

3 tablespoons unsweetened
    plant-based milk

75 g (3 oz) Cheddar-style vegan
    cheese, grated

salt and pepper

For 14 g more protein, add 150 g (5 oz) fresh or frozen peas, 90 g (3¼ oz) broccoli florets and 60 g (2¼ oz) chopped kale, steamed, per serving.

Heat the olive oil in a saucepan, add the onion, carrot, celery and thyme and cook gently for 10 minutes until soft and golden.

Crumble in the plant-based mince and cook over a medium-high heat, breaking it up with a wooden spoon and stirring frequently, for about 10 minutes until browned. Add the tomatoes, tomato purée and salt and pepper to taste. Bring to the boil, then reduce the heat, cover and simmer for 30 minutes.

Remove the lid and cook for a further 15 minutes until thickened.

Meanwhile, put the potatoes in a large saucepan of lightly salted water and bring to the boil. Reduce the heat and simmer for 15–20 minutes until really tender. Drain well and return to the pan. Mash in the vegan butter, plant-based milk and half the vegan cheese and season to taste with salt and pepper.

Transfer the plant-based mince mixture to a 2 litre (3½ pint) baking dish and carefully spoon the mash over the top, spreading over the surface of the filling. Fork the top of the mash and scatter over the remaining vegan cheese. Bake in a preheated oven, 190°C (375°F), Gas Mark 5, for 20–25 minutes until bubbling and golden.

Pad Thai

30 MINUTES					
2 SERVINGS					

578	KCAL / SERVING	3 G	FIBRE
26 G	PROTEIN	4 G	SUGAR
25 G	FAT	3 G	SAT FAT
60 G	CARBS	1223 MG	SODIUM

125 g (4 oz) dried rice noodles

½ tablespoons sweet soy sauce

½ tablespoon lime juice

1 tablespoon vegan fish sauce

1 tablespoon water

1 tablespoon groundnut oil

2 garlic cloves, sliced

1 small red chilli, deseeded
    and chopped

125 g (4 oz) firm tofu, drained,
    patted dry and diced

90 g (3¼ oz) liquid vegan egg
    replacement

125 g (4 oz) bean sprouts

1 tablespoon chopped fresh coriander

2 tablespoons chopped salted,
    roasted peanuts

Cook the noodles in a saucepan of boiling water for 5 minutes until softened. Drain and immediately refresh under cold water, drain again and set aside.

Mix together the sweet soy sauce, lime juice, vegan fish sauce and measured water in a small bowl and set aside.

Heat the groundnut oil in a wok or large frying pan, add the garlic and chilli and stir-fry over a medium heat for 30 seconds. Add the noodles and tofu and stir-fry for 2–3 minutes until heated through.

Carefully push the noodle mixture up the side of the pan, clearing the centre of the pan. Add the egg replacement and heat gently for 1 minute without stirring, then gently start 'scrambling' the egg replacement with a spoon. Mix the noodle mixture back into the centre of the pan and stir well until mixed with the eggs.

Add the soy sauce mixture and cook for 1 minute or until heated through. Stir in the bean sprouts and coriander. Spoon into warm bowls and serve immediately, topped with the peanuts.

For 13 g more protein per serving, swap the bean sprouts for 125 g (4 oz) frozen shelled edamame beans, precooked in a saucepan of boiling water for 3 minutes, then drained.

Plant-based Sausage Meatballs, Peas & Pasta

40 MINUTES

4 SERVINGS

608	KCAL / SERVING	5 G	FIBRE
27 G	PROTEIN	6 G	SUGAR
19 G	FAT	3 G	SAT FAT
90 G	CARBS	833 MG	SODIUM

8 plant-based sausages, about 300 g (10 oz) in total, skins removed, or 250 g (8 oz) dried plant-based sausage mix, reconstituted according to the pack instructions

plain flour, for dusting (optional)

2 tablespoons extra virgin olive oil

400 g (13 oz) dried fusilli

250 g (8 oz) frozen peas, defrosted

2 garlic cloves, sliced

2 tablespoons chopped sage

½ teaspoon dried chilli flakes

salt and pepper

25 g (1 oz) Parmesan-style vegan cheese, grated, to serve

Cut the plant-based sausage meat into small pieces and roll with slightly wet or floured hands into walnut-sized meatballs.

Heat half the oil in a large nonstick frying pan, add the meatballs and cook over a medium heat, stirring frequently, for 10 minutes until browned and cooked through. Remove from the pan with a slotted spoon.

Meanwhile, cook the fusilli in a large saucepan of lightly salted boiling water for 8 minutes. Add the peas, return to the boil and cook for a further 2 minutes until the peas are just tender and the pasta is al dente. Drain well, reserving 4 tablespoons of the cooking water.

Add the garlic, sage, chilli flakes and salt and pepper to taste to the meatball pan and cook over a low heat for 2–3 minutes until the garlic is soft but not browned. Return the meatballs to the pan.

Return the pasta and peas to their pan and stir in the meatball mixture, the reserved pasta cooking water and remaining oil and heat through for 2 minutes. Serve in warm bowls sprinkled with the grated Parmesan-style vegan cheese.

For a high-protein homemade Parmesan-style vegan cheese (an extra 12 g per serving), mix 4 tablespoons hulled hemp seeds with 4 tablespoons nutritional yeast flakes and a pinch of salt.

Spicy Bean Burgers

35 MINUTES				
4 SERVINGS	594	KCAL / SERVING	17 G	FIBRE
	28 G	PROTEIN	11 G	SUGAR
	16 G	FAT	3 G	SAT FAT
	88 G	CARBS	1658 MG	SODIUM

1 tablespoon sunflower oil

1 onion, finely chopped

1 green chilli, deseeded and
finely chopped

2 teaspoons Mexican or fajita
spice mix

2 x 400 g (13 oz) cans red kidney beans,
rinsed and drained

100 g (3½ oz) fresh white breadcrumbs

4 tablespoons chopped
fresh coriander

45 g (1¾ oz) liquid vegan egg
replacement or 1 tablespoon
ground flaxseeds mixed with
3 tablespoons hot water

2 teaspoons chipotle paste

salt and pepper

TO SERVE

4 seeded burger buns

145 g (4¾ oz) crisp green lettuce

4 tablespoons ready-made fresh
tomato salsa

125 g (4 oz) ready-made guacamole

Heat the sunflower oil in a small frying pan, add the onion and chilli and cook over a medium heat for 2–3 minutes until softened. Stir in the spice mix and cook, stirring, for 1 minute. Leave to cool slightly.

Mash the beans in a large bowl with a potato masher or fork, then add the breadcrumbs and coriander and season well with salt and pepper.

Beat the egg replacement with the chipotle paste in a small bowl, then add to the bean mixture and mix together well with a fork. Divide the bean mixture into 4 equal portions, using slightly wet hands, then shape each portion into a burger.

Place the burgers on a nonstick baking sheet and cook under a preheated medium-hot grill for 4–5 minutes on each side until golden and cooked through.

Split the buns in half horizontally. Top the bottom halves of the buns with the lettuce and a tablespoonful of salsa. Place the burgers on top and finish with a tablespoonful of guacamole. Cover with the top halves of the buns and serve.

Spinach, Tomato & Tofu Curry

45 MINUTES			
4 SERVINGS			

486	KCAL / SERVING	6 G	FIBRE
29 G	PROTEIN	6 G	SUGAR
22 G	FAT	8 G	SAT FAT
44 G	CARBS	447 MG	SODIUM

500 g (1 lb) spinach leaves

40 g (1½ oz) vegan butter

2 teaspoons cumin seeds

1 red chilli, deseeded and
finely chopped

1 onion, very finely chopped

2 plum tomatoes, finely chopped

2 teaspoons finely grated garlic

1 tablespoon peeled and finely
grated fresh root ginger

1 teaspoon chilli powder

1 teaspoon ground coriander

500 g (1 lb) pressed firm tofu,
cut into bite-sized pieces

2 tablespoons plant-based
single cream

1 teaspoon lemon juice

2 tablespoons finely chopped
fresh coriander leaves

salt and pepper

160 g (5½ oz) brown rice, cooked,
to serve

Cook the spinach in a large saucepan of boiling water for 2–3 minutes, then drain well. Transfer to a blender or food processor and blend to a smooth purée, then set aside.

Heat 25 g (1 oz) of the vegan butter in a large wok or frying pan, add the cumin seeds, red chilli and onion and stir-fry over a medium-low heat for 6–8 minutes until the onion has softened. Add the tomatoes, garlic, ginger, chilli powder and ground coriander and season well with salt and pepper. Stir through and cook for 2–3 minutes. Remove the tomato mixture from the pan and set aside.

Wipe out the pan, then melt the remaining vegan butter, add the tofu and stir-fry over a medium-high heat for about 10 minutes until browned on all sides. Add the spinach purée, return the tomato mixture to the pan and stir-fry for 4–5 minutes until well mixed and heated through.

Remove the pan from the heat and stir in the plant-based cream, lemon juice and chopped coriander. Spoon into warm bowls and serve with brown rice, cooked according to the pack instructions.

*For an extra 8 g protein,
add ½ warm flatbread
per serving.*

Veggie Sausage Hotpot

50 MINUTES		

646	KCAL / SERVING	12 G	FIBRE
33 G	PROTEIN	8 G	SUGAR
25 G	FAT	7 G	SAT FAT
80 G	CARBS	1292 MG	SODIUM

4 SERVINGS

40 g (1½ oz) vegan butter, softened

1 tablespoon olive oil

8 plant-based sausages, about
   300 g (10 oz) in total

100 g (3½ oz) chestnut mushrooms,
   trimmed and sliced

1 red onion, sliced

200 g (7 oz) dried Puy lentils, rinsed
   and drained

400 ml (13 fl oz) vegan vegetable stock

2 tablespoons chopped oregano

2 tablespoons sun-dried tomato paste

300 g (10 oz) cherry tomatoes, halved

1 garlic clove, crushed

2 tablespoons chopped flat
   leaf parsley

8 small or 4 large slices of ciabatta

salt and pepper

Melt half the vegan butter with the olive oil in a sauté pan or flameproof casserole dish with a lid, add the plant-based sausages with the mushrooms and onion and cook for a few minutes, turning frequently, until lightly browned.

Add the lentils, stock, oregano and tomato paste and mix the ingredients together. Bring to the boil and cover with the lid, then reduce the heat and cook very gently for about 20 minutes until the lentils are tender and the stock is nearly all absorbed.

Stir in the tomatoes and season to taste with salt and pepper. Cook for a further 5 minutes.

Meanwhile, mix the garlic and parsley with the remaining vegan butter in a small bowl, then spread thinly over the ciabatta slices.

Arrange over the hotpot and cook under a preheated medium grill for about 5 minutes until the bread is lightly toasted. Serve immediately.

Vegan Bacon, Chorizo & Tomato Linguine

45
MINUTES

4
SERVINGS

581	KCAL / SERVING	13 G	FIBRE
35 G	PROTEIN	11 G	SUGAR
28 G	FAT	3 G	SAT FAT
53 G	CARBS	546 MG	SODIUM

250 g (8 oz) plant-based bacon bits

2 teaspoons mild paprika

salt and pepper

250 g (8 oz) dried linguine

5 tablespoons olive oil

50 g (2 oz) plant-based chorizo-style
    sausage, diced

1 red onion, sliced

250 g (8 oz) passata

3 tablespoons sun-dried tomato paste

½ teaspoon saffron threads

250 ml (8 fl oz) vegan vegetable stock

50 g (2 oz) fresh or frozen peas

3 garlic cloves, crushed

4 tablespoons chopped flat
    leaf parsley

finely grated zest of 1 lemon

Toss the plant-based bacon bits in the paprika and some salt and pepper. Roll up half the pasta in a clean tea towel. Run the tea towel firmly over the edge of a work surface so that you hear the pasta breaking into short lengths. Transfer to a bowl. Break up the remaining pasta in the same way.

Heat 3 tablespoons of the olive oil in a large frying pan, add the plant-based bacon bits and chorizo-style sausage along with the onion and cook very gently, stirring frequently, for about 10 minutes until browned. Stir in the passata, tomato paste, saffron and stock and bring to the boil.

Reduce the heat, sprinkle in the pasta and stir well to mix. Cook gently, stirring frequently, for 10 minutes until the pasta is tender, adding a little water to the pan if the mixture becomes dry before the pasta is cooked. Add the peas and cook for a further 3 minutes.

Stir in the garlic, parsley, lemon zest and remaining oil. Check the seasoning and serve.

For Vegan Chicken & Tomato Linguine

Follow the recipe above, using 300 g (10 oz) plant-based chicken pieces instead of the plant-based bacon bits. Toss in the paprika and salt and pepper and cook with the plant-based chorizo-style sausage and onion as above, but swap the peas for broad beans and the parsley for basil.

Tasty Sweet Treats

Banana & Pecan Loaf

1¼ HOURS			
8 SERVINGS			

509	KCAL / SERVING	4 G	FIBRE
17 G	PROTEIN	23 G	SUGAR
27 G	FAT	8 G	SAT FAT
53 G	CARBS	383 MG	SODIUM

125 g (4 oz) vegan butter, softened, plus extra for greasing

125 g (4 oz) soft light brown sugar

90 g (3¼ oz) liquid vegan egg replacement

4 ripe bananas, mashed

100 ml (3½ fl oz) soya milk

225 g (7½ oz) plain flour

125 g (4 oz) vegan vanilla protein powder

1 teaspoon bicarbonate of soda

1 teaspoon baking powder

½ teaspoon salt

125 g (4 oz) pecan nuts, roughly chopped, plus 8 halves to decorate

Grease a 1 kg (2 lb) loaf tin.

Beat the vegan butter and sugar together in a large bowl with a hand-held electric whisk until pale and fluffy. Beat in the egg replacement, mashed bananas and soya milk until well combined.

Sift over the flour, protein powder, bicarbonate of soda, baking powder and salt and gently fold in with a large metal spoon, then stir in the chopped pecan nuts.

Spoon the mixture into the prepared tin and arrange the pecan halves down the centre.

Bake in a preheated oven, 180°C (350°F), Gas Mark 4, for 50–60 minutes or until risen and golden brown and a skewer inserted into the centre comes out clean. Cover the top of the loaf with foil if it becomes too brown.

Leave the loaf to cool in the tin for a few minutes, then turn out on to a wire rack to cool completely before serving.

For 5 g more protein per serving, serve with 175 g (6 oz) plant-based vanilla custard. ➝

For Banana, Sultana & Walnut Bread

Make the mixture as above, using 125 g (4 oz) chopped walnuts in place of the pecans and stirring in 125 g (4 oz) sultanas with the nuts. Arrange 8 walnut halves down the centre of the loaf and bake as above.

Chilli Chocolate Chip Cakes

40 MINUTES

8 SERVINGS

414	KCAL / CAKE	3 G	FIBRE
9 G	PROTEIN	22 G	SUGAR
22 G	FAT	8 G	SAT FAT
47 G	CARBS	110 MG	SODIUM

200 g (7 oz) self-raising flour

50 g (2 oz) cocoa powder

1 teaspoon baking powder

150 g (5 oz) soft light brown sugar

250 ml (8 fl oz) soya milk

90 g (3¼ oz) liquid vegan egg
   replacement

50 g (2 oz) vegan butter, melted

125 g (4 oz) vegan chilli chocolate
   or vegan plain dark chocolate with
   a pinch of chilli powder, chopped

75 g (3 oz) pecan nuts, toasted and
   roughly ground

olive oil spray, for oiling

Cut a 15 cm (6 inch) square from nonstick baking paper and use it as a template to cut 7 more. Fold each square into quarters. Open out flat and set aside.

Sift the flour, cocoa powder and baking powder into a bowl and stir in the sugar. In a separate bowl, mix together the soya milk, egg replacement and melted vegan butter. Add to the flour mixture and mix together with a fork until only just combined. Fold in the chocolate and pecan nuts.

Spray each square of baking paper with olive oil spray and press each piece into the cup of a muffin tin. Spoon the chocolate mixture into the lined cups and bake in a preheated oven, 200°C (400°F), Gas Mark 6, for 20 minutes until the cakes are risen and golden. Leave to cool slightly on a wire rack and serve warm.

Double Chocolate Puddings

40 MINUTES				
6 SERVINGS	513	KCAL / PUDDING	4 G	FIBRE
	6 G	PROTEIN	28 G	SUGAR
	33 G	FAT	17 G	SAT FAT
	48 G	CARBS	40 MG	SODIUM

125 g (4 oz) unsalted vegan butter, softened, plus extra for greasing

125 g (4 oz) light muscovado sugar

100 g (3½ oz) self-raising flour

15 g (½ oz) cocoa powder

45 g (1¾ oz) liquid vegan egg replacement

75 g (3 oz) or 12 squares vegan plain dark chocolate

100 g (3 ½ oz) vegan white chocolate, broken into pieces

150 ml (¼ pint) plant-based double or single cream

¼ teaspoon vanilla extract

For 4 g more protein per pudding, swap the white chocolate cream for 125 g (4 oz) warmed soya chocolate dessert per serving. →

Grease a deep 6-cup muffin tin. Put the vegan butter, sugar, flour, cocoa and egg replacement in a bowl and beat with a hand-held electric whisk for about 1 minute until pale and creamy.

Divide the mixture between the greased cups of the muffin tin, then press 2 squares of dark chocolate into each and cover with the mixture.

Bake in a preheated oven, 180°C (350°F), Gas Mark 4, for 18–20 minutes until the puddings are well risen, slightly crusty around the edges and the centre springs back when pressed with a fingertip.

Meanwhile, warm together the white chocolate, cream and vanilla extract in a small saucepan, stirring until the chocolate has completely melted.

Loosen the edges of the baked puddings with a round-bladed knife, then turn out and transfer to shallow serving bowls. Drizzle with the white chocolate cream and serve immediately.

For Walnut & Chocolate Puddings

Beat the vegan butter, sugar and egg replacement as above with 125 g (4 oz) self-raising flour and 2 teaspoons instant coffee dissolved in 3 teaspoons boiling water until pale and creamy, then stir in 50 g (2 oz) roughly chopped walnuts. Divide the mixture between the greased cups of the muffin tin and add the dark chocolate squares, then bake as above. Serve with 250 ml (8 fl oz) soya cream.

Frosted Banana Bars

1
HOUR, PLUS
SETTING

16
SERVINGS

317	KCAL / BAR	0 G	FIBRE
8 G	PROTEIN	29 G	SUGAR
13 G	FAT	7 G	SAT FAT
42 G	CARBS	64 MG	SODIUM

175 g (6 oz) vegan butter, softened

175 g (6 oz) caster sugar

135 g (4½ oz) liquid vegan egg
   replacement

2 bananas, about 175 g (6 oz) each
   with skins on, roughly mashed

100 ml (3½ fl oz) soya milk

250 g (8 oz) self-raising flour

120 g (4 oz) vegan protein powder

1 teaspoon baking powder

sugar shapes and sprinkles,
   to decorate (optional)

CHOCOLATE ICING

50 g (2 oz) vegan butter

25 g (1 oz) cocoa powder

250 g (8 oz) icing sugar, sifted

1–2 tablespoons soya milk

Line an 18 x 28 cm (7 x 11 inch) roasting tin with nonstick baking paper. Beat the vegan butter and sugar together in a large bowl with a hand-held electric whisk until pale and fluffy. Beat in the egg replacement, mashed bananas and soya milk until well combined.

Sift over the flour, protein powder and baking powder and gently fold in with a large metal spoon.

Spoon the mixture into the lined tin and level the surface. Bake in a preheated oven, 180°C (350°F), Gas Mark 4, for 25–30 minutes until the cake is well risen, golden and springs back when gently pressed with a fingertip. Leave to cool completely in the tin.

For the icing, heat the vegan butter in a saucepan. Stir in the cocoa and cook gently for 1 minute. Remove the pan from the heat and mix in the icing sugar. Return to the heat and heat gently, stirring, until melted and smooth, adding enough soya milk to mix to a smooth spreadable icing.

Pour the icing over the top of the cake and spread smoothly over the surface. Sprinkle with sugar shapes and sprinkles, if liked, and leave the icing to cool and set.

Lift the cake out of the tin using the lining paper. Cut into 16 bars and peel off the paper. Store in an airtight container for up to 3 days.

Steamed Apple Pudding

644	KCAL / SERVING	
9 G	PROTEIN	
28 G	FAT	
91 G	CARBS	

4 G	FIBRE
50 G	SUGAR
14 G	SAT FAT
128 MG	SODIUM

2¼ HOURS, PLUS COOLING

4 SERVINGS

4 tablespoons golden syrup

2 cooking apples, about 500 g (1 lb) in total, peeled and cored, 1 thickly sliced, 1 coarsely grated

125 g (4 oz) unsalted vegan butter, softened, plus extra for greasing

100 g (3½ oz) caster sugar

90 g (3¼ oz) liquid vegan egg replacement

200 g (7 oz) self-raising flour

finely grated zest of 1 orange and 3 tablespoons of the juice

Grease a 1.2 litre (2 pint) pudding basin lightly and line the base with a small circle of nonstick baking paper.

Spoon the golden syrup into the prepared basin, then arrange the sliced apple in an even layer on top.

Put the vegan butter, sugar, egg replacement and flour in a bowl and beat with a hand-held electric whisk for about 1 minute until pale and creamy. Stir in the grated apple and orange zest and juice.

Spoon the pudding mixture into the basin and level the surface. Cover with a piece of pleated nonstick baking paper and foil. Tie in place under the rim with string, adding a string handle.

Lower the basin into the top of a steamer set over a saucepan of simmering water, or into a large saucepan and then half-fill the pan with boiling water. Cover with a tight-fitting lid and steam gently for 2 hours until the pudding is well risen and a knife comes out clean when inserted into the centre, topping up the water as necessary. Leave to stand for 10 minutes.

Remove the foil and paper, loosen the edge of the pudding with a round-bladed knife and invert on to a serving plate with a rim. Serve immediately.

For 5 g more protein per serving, serve with 150 g (5 oz) shop-bought vanilla soya custard.

For Cranberry & Orange Steamed Pudding

Cook 150 g (5 oz) frozen cranberries in a saucepan with the orange juice for 5 minutes until softened. Spoon 2 tablespoons raspberry jam into a pudding basin prepared as opposite, then add the cranberries. Make the pudding mixture as opposite, finishing with the grated cooking apple and the orange zest. Cover and steam as opposite.

For Spotted Dick

Warm 3 tablespoons orange juice or rum in a small saucepan, add 150 g (5 oz) raisins, 1 teaspoon ground ginger and ¼ teaspoon grated nutmeg and leave to soak for 1 hour or longer. Add to the flour mixture as opposite just before adding the egg replacement and soya milk. Knead the dough lightly, then simply shape into a long sausage (omitting the jam and raspberries), wrap in nonstick baking paper and foil and bake in the oven as opposite. Serve in slices with 450 g (14½ oz) plant-based custard, flavoured with a little extra rum if liked.

Jam Roly-poly

2½ HOURS	
6 SERVINGS	

508	KCAL / SERVING	4 G	FIBRE
10 G	PROTEIN	25 G	SUGAR
19 G	FAT	8 G	SAT FAT
75 G	CARBS	155 MG	SODIUM

300 g (10 oz) self-raising flour,
   plus extra for dusting
1 teaspoon baking powder
150 g (5 oz) shredded vegetable suet
75 g (3 oz) caster sugar
50 g (2 oz) fresh breadcrumbs
finely grated zest of 1 lemon
finely grated zest of 1 orange
45 g (1¾ oz) vegan egg replacement
175–200 ml (6–7 fl oz) soya milk,
   plus extra for brushing
6 tablespoons raspberry jam
150 g (5 oz) frozen raspberries,
   just defrosted

Put the flour, baking powder, suet and sugar in a large bowl, then stir in the breadcrumbs and citrus zest. Add the egg replacement, then gradually mix in enough soya milk to make a soft but not sticky dough.

Knead the dough lightly on a lightly floured surface, then roll out into a 30 cm (12 inch) square. Spread with the raspberry jam, leaving a 2.5 cm (1 inch) border, then sprinkle the raspberries on top. Brush the border with a little soya milk, then roll up the dough. Wrap loosely in a large piece of nonstick baking paper, twisting the edges together and leaving a little space for the pudding to rise, then wrap loosely in foil.

Place on a roasting rack set over a large roasting tin, then pour boiling water into the tin but not over the roasting rack. Cover the tin with foil and twist over the edges to seal well. Bake in a preheated oven, 150°C (300°F), Gas Mark 2, for 2 hours until the pudding is well risen. Check once or twice during baking and top up the water as necessary.

Transfer the pudding to a chopping board using a tea towel. Unwrap, cut into thick slices and serve hot.

For 3 g protein more per serving, make your own vanilla soya custard. Pour 450 ml (¾ pint) soya milk into a saucepan and stir in 2 tablespoons caster sugar, 2 teaspoons vanilla extract and a pinch of ground turmeric for colour. Warm over a gentle heat. Mix 6 tablespoons cold soya milk with 3 tablespoons cornflour in a small bowl until smooth. Add to the custard mixture and cook, stirring frequently, until the mixture thickens.

Rice Pudding
with Drunken Raisins

2¼ HOURS, PLUS SOAKING					
	226	KCAL / SERVING	0 G	FIBRE	
	6 G	• PROTEIN	14 G	SUGAR	
4 SERVINGS	8 G	FAT	3 G	SAT FAT	
	33 G	CARBS	108 MG	SODIUM	

50 g (2 oz) raisins

2 tablespoons fortified wine, such as
   sweet sherry or Madeira

65 g (2½ oz) pudding rice

25 g (1 oz) caster sugar

600 ml (1 pint) soya milk

25 g (1 oz) unsalted vegan butter,
   diced, plus extra for greasing

large pinch each of grated nutmeg
   and ground cinnamon

4 tablespoons soya single cream,
   to serve

Put the raisins in a small saucepan with the fortified wine and warm together, or microwave in a small bowl for 30 seconds on full power. Leave to soak for 30 minutes, or longer if time allows.

Grease a 900 ml (1½ pint) pie dish, then add the rice and the sugar. Spoon the soaked raisins on top, then cover with the soya milk. Dot with the vegan butter and sprinkle with the spices.

Cook in a preheated oven, 150°C (300°F), Gas Mark 2, for 2 hours until the pudding is golden on top, the rice is tender and the soya milk thick and creamy. Spoon into bowls and top each serving with a tablespoonful of the soya cream.

For High-protein Quinoa Pudding

Rinse 90 g (3¼ oz) quinoa until the water runs clear, then drain. Put in a saucepan with the sugar, soya milk, nutmeg and cinnamon as above, plus a small pinch of salt. Bring to the boil over a medium heat. Reduce the heat, cover but leave a little gap for some steam to escape and simmer gently for 25 minutes, stirring about every 5 minutes. Remove the lid and simmer for a further 5 minutes until thick. Remove from heat, stir in 1 tablespoon vanilla extract and serve.

Spiced Pear & Cranberry Muffins

40				
MINUTES, PLUS SOAKING	240	KCAL / MUFFIN	2 G	FIBRE
	5 G	PROTEIN	15 G	SUGAR
12	9 G	FAT	2 G	SAT FAT
SERVINGS	37 G	CARBS	163 MG	SODIUM

40 g (1½ oz) dried cranberries

2 tablespoons boiling water

300 g (10 oz) plain flour

3 teaspoons baking powder

1 teaspoon ground cinnamon

½ teaspoon grated nutmeg

125 g (4 oz) caster sugar, plus extra
for sprinkling

150 ml (¼ pint) plant-based
natural yogurt

135 g (4½ oz) liquid vegan egg
replacement

50 g (2 oz) vegan butter, melted

3 tablespoons olive oil

3 small ripe pears, peeled, cored
and diced

Line a 12-cup muffin tin with paper muffin cases.

Put the cranberries in a cup, add the measured boiling water and leave to soak for 10 minutes.

Mix together the flour, baking powder, spices and sugar in a large bowl. In a separate bowl, mix together the plant-based yogurt, egg replacement, melted vegan butter and olive oil. Add to the flour mixture and mix together with a fork until only just combined.

Drain the cranberries and fold into the flour mixture with the pears.

Divide the mixture between the muffin cases and sprinkle with a little extra sugar. Bake in a preheated oven, 200°C (400°F), Gas Mark 6, for 15–18 minutes until the muffins are well risen and golden. Leave to cool in the tin for 5 minutes, then transfer to a wire rack. Serve warm or cold.

For Blueberry & Cranberry Muffins

Soak the dried cranberries and make the muffin mixture as above, omitting the pears and spices and adding 125 g (4 oz) fresh blueberries and the grated zest of 1 lemon along with the drained cranberries. Bake and serve as above.

Steamed Pudding with Mango

2 HOURS, PLUS STANDING	449	KCAL / SERVING		2 G	FIBRE	
	7 G	PROTEIN		31 G	SUGAR	
6 SERVINGS	23 G	FAT		13 G	SAT FAT	
	55 G	CARBS		63 MG	SODIUM	

1 ripe mango, peeled, stoned and cut into chunks

2 tablespoons vanilla syrup, plus extra to serve

125 g (4 oz) unsalted vegan butter, softened, plus extra for greasing

125 g (4 oz) caster sugar

1 teaspoon vanilla extract

90 g (3¼ oz) liquid vegan egg replacement

175 g (6 oz) self-raising flour

4 tablespoons unsweetened desiccated coconut

1 tablespoon soya milk

Grease a 1.2 litre (2 pint) pudding basin lightly and line the base with a circle of nonstick baking paper.

Scatter the mango chunks into the prepared basin and drizzle with the vanilla syrup.

Put the vegan butter, sugar, vanilla extract, egg replacement and flour in a bowl and beat with a hand-held electric whisk for about 1 minute until pale and creamy. Stir in the coconut and soya milk.

Spoon the mixture into the basin and level the surface. Cover with a piece of pleated nonstick baking paper and foil. Tie in place under the rim with string, adding a string handle.

Lower the basin into the top of a steamer set over a saucepan of simmering water, or into a large saucepan and then half-fill the pan with boiling water. Cover with a tight-fitting lid and steam gently for 1 hour 40 minutes until the pudding is well risen and a knife comes out clean when inserted into the centre, topping up the water as necessary. Leave to stand for 10 minutes.

Remove the foil and paper, loosen the edge of the pudding with a round-bladed knife and invert on to a serving plate. Drizzle with extra vanilla syrup and serve.

For 5 g more protein per serving, serve with 150 g (5 oz) shop-bought vanilla soya custard, or make your own for 3 g more protein (see page 125).

Peanut Butter Cookies

20 MINUTES

12 COOKIES

239	KCAL / SERVING	2 G	FIBRE
11 G	PROTEIN	17 G	SUGAR
13 G	FAT	4 G	SAT FAT
20 G	CARBS	162 MG	SODIUM

250 g (8 oz) smooth peanut butter

150 g (5 oz) light soft brown sugar

45 g (1¾ oz) liquid vegan egg replacement

115 g (3¾ oz) vanilla vegan protein powder

45 g (1¾ oz) vegan plain dark chocolate chips

Line an 26 x 35 cm (10 x 13¾ inch) roasting tin with nonstick baking paper.

Mix the peanut butter, brown sugar, vegan egg replacement, protein powder and chocolate chips by hand in a bowl until combined.

Form 12 balls of cookie dough and space them evenly on the baking paper. Press down on each ball to form a cookie shape.

Bake in a preheated oven, 190°C (375°F), Gas Mark 5, for 12–14 minutes, or until the edges begin to brown.

Leave to cool for 2 minutes, then transfer to a wire rack to cool completely.

Apple Fritters
with Blackberry Sauce

25 MINUTES		
4 SERVINGS		

412	KCAL / SERVING	7 G	FIBRE
9 G	PROTEIN	34 G	SUGAR
14 G	FAT	1 G	SAT FAT
65 G	CARBS	88 MG	SODIUM

125 g (4 oz) plain flour

4 tablespoons caster sugar

90 g (3¼ oz) liquid vegan egg replacement

150 ml (¼ pint) soya milk

sunflower oil, for deep-frying

4 dessert apples, cored and thickly sliced

150 g (5 oz) frozen blackberries

2 tablespoons water

icing sugar, for dusting

Sift the flour into a bowl and stir in 2 tablespoons of the sugar. Add the egg replacement, then gradually whisk in the soya milk to make a smooth batter.

Pour the oil for deep-frying into a deep, heavy-based saucepan until it comes one-third of the way up the side, then heat until it reaches 180–190°C (350–375°F) or until a cube of bread browns in 30 seconds. Dip a few apple slices in the batter and turn gently to coat. Lift out one slice at a time and lower carefully into the hot oil. Deep-fry, in batches, for 2–3 minutes, turning until evenly golden. Remove with a slotted spoon and drain on kitchen paper.

Meanwhile, put the blackberries, remaining sugar and the measured water in a small saucepan and heat for 2–3 minutes until heated through and the sugar has dissolved.

Arrange the fritters on serving plates, spoon the blackberry sauce around and dust with a little icing sugar.

For Banana Fritters with Raspberry Sauce

Make the batter and use to coat 4 thickly sliced bananas, then deep-fry, in batches, as above. Meanwhile, make a sauce using 150 g (5 oz) raspberries with the sugar and water as above, then serve with the banana fritters.

Warm Pecan Caramel Cupcakes

40 MINUTES

12 SERVINGS

359	KCAL / SERVING	1 G	FIBRE
10 G	PROTEIN	20 G	SUGAR
22 G	FAT	10 G	SAT FAT
31 G	CARBS	82 MG	SODIUM

125 g (4 oz) lightly salted vegan butter, softened

125 g (4 oz) light muscovado sugar

90 g (3¼ oz) liquid vegan egg replacement

150 g (5 oz) self-raising flour

125 g (4 oz) vegan vanilla protein powder

½ teaspoon baking powder

75 g (3 oz) pecan nuts, roughly chopped, plus extra to decorate (optional)

250 g (8 oz) caramel sauce (see below for homemade)

Line a 12-cup cupcake tin with paper cupcake cases.

Put the vegan butter, sugar, egg replacement, flour, protein powder and baking powder in a bowl and beat with a hand-held electric whisk for about 1 minute until pale and creamy. Stir in the pecan nuts.

Divide the cake mixture between the cupcake cases. Bake in a preheated oven, 180°C (350°F), Gas Mark 4, for 20 minutes or until the cupcakes are risen and just firm to the touch. Transfer to a wire rack.

Heat the caramel sauce in a small saucepan over a medium heat, stirring gently until melted but not boiling. Drizzle the sauce over the cakes while still warm and scatter with the remaining pecan nuts, if liked. You may want to take the cupcakes out of their cases to serve.

For Homemade Caramel Sauce

Put 200 g (7 oz) caster sugar in a small saucepan with 75 ml (3 fl oz) water and heat very gently, stirring, until the sugar has dissolved. Bring to the boil and boil rapidly, without stirring, until the syrup turns to a pale caramel colour (watch closely, as the syrup will quickly overbrown). Remove from the heat and stir in 50 g (2 oz) salted vegan butter and 150 ml (¼ pint) plant-based single cream. Return to the heat and cook, stirring, until smooth. Drizzle the sauce over the warm cupcakes as above.

Red Rice Risotto & Sautéed Grapes

1¼ HOURS				
486	KCAL / SERVING	3 G	FIBRE
11 G	PROTEIN	24 G	SUGAR
22 G	FAT	10 G	SAT FAT
62 G	CARBS	2 MG	SODIUM

4 SERVINGS

75 g (3 oz) unsalted vegan butter

175 g (6 oz) Camargue red rice, rinsed and drained

750–900 ml (1¼–1½ pints) soya milk

½ teaspoon ground mixed spice, plus a little extra to decorate

50 g (2 oz) light muscovado sugar

250 g (8 oz) red seedless grapes, halved

50 g (2 oz) oat crème fraîche

Heat 50 g (2 oz) of the vegan butter in a saucepan, add the rice and cook gently for 2 minutes, stirring. In a separate saucepan, heat the soya milk, then pour about one-third over the rice and add the mixed spice.

Cook gently for 40–50 minutes, stirring occasionally, adding ladlefuls of the remaining soya milk as the rice swells. Stir more frequently towards the end of the cooking time, until all the soya milk has all been incorporated and the rice is tender and creamy. Remove the pan from the heat and stir in the sugar.

Heat the remaining vegan butter in a frying pan, add the grapes and fry for 2–3 minutes until hot.

Spoon the risotto into shallow bowls and top with a spoonful of oat crème fraîche, then spoon over the grapes and sprinkle with a little extra mixed spice. Serve immediately.

For Cherry Risotto

Heat 50 g (2 oz) vegan butter in a saucepan, add 175 g (6 oz) risotto rice and cook gently for 2 minutes, stirring. Warm 600–750 ml (1–1¼ pints) soya milk with 50 g (2 oz) dried cherries and 1 teaspoon vanilla extract in a separate saucepan. Add about one-third to the rice and cook gently for 20–25 minutes, gradually adding the remaining soya milk mixture as above until the rice is tender and creamy. Stir in 50 g (2 oz) caster sugar, then serve the risotto topped with a tablespoonful of oat crème fraîche per serving.

For Brazil Nut & Orange Cupcakes

Simmer 1 small orange as opposite until soft and squashy. Drain and leave to cool, then put in a blender or food processor with the egg replacement, melted vegan butter, agave nectar or sugar and sultanas as opposite and blend to a purée. Chop and then grind 100 g (3½ oz) Brazil nuts in a food processor. Mix with the flour, vanilla vegan protein powder and baking powder as opposite, adding ½ teaspoon ground allspice (omit the poppy seeds). Stir in the orange purée mixture and bake as opposite, with a whole Brazil nut on top of each cupcake.

Poppy Seed & Lemon Cupcakes

1¼ HOURS, PLUS COOLING	177	KCAL / CUPCAKE	2 G	FIBRE
	6 G	PROTEIN	9 G	SUGAR
12 SERVINGS	13 G	FAT	3 G	SAT FAT
	14 G	CARBS	84 MG	SODIUM

2 lemons, 1 cut into 12 thin slices, 1 kept whole

135 g (4½ oz) vegan egg replacement

5 tablespoons agave nectar or caster sugar, plus extra agave nectar for drizzling

75 g (3 oz) lightly salted vegan butter, melted

100 g (3½ oz) ground hazelnuts

50 g (2 oz) spelt flour

2 tablespoons vanilla vegan protein powder

1 teaspoon baking powder

2 tablespoons poppy seeds

50 g (2 oz) sultanas

Line a 12-cup cupcake tin with paper cupcake cases.

Put the lemon slices and whole lemon in a small saucepan and cover with boiling water. Simmer very gently for 20–30 minutes until the slices are tender. Lift out the slices with a slotted spoon and set aside. Cook the whole lemon for a further 15 minutes until soft and squashy. Drain and leave to cool.

Halve the whole lemon and discard the pips. Roughly chop, put in a blender or food processor and blend to a purée. Transfer to a bowl. Add the egg replacement, agave nectar or sugar and melted vegan butter and mix together well.

In a separate bowl, mix together the ground hazelnuts, flour, protein powder, baking powder and poppy seeds. Add the lemon purée mixture with the sultanas and stir until evenly combined.

Divide the cake mixture between the cupcake cases. Place a reserved lemon slice on top of each and drizzle with a little extra agave nectar.

Bake in a preheated oven, 180°C (350°F), Gas Mark 4, for 20 minutes or until the cupcakes are risen and lightly browned. Transfer to a wire rack and leave to cool completely.

Glossary of UK/US terms

UK	US
baking tin	baking pan
bicarbonate of soda	baking soda
black treacle	blackstrap molasses
broad beans	fava beans
butter beans	lima beans
cases	liners
caster sugar	superfine sugar
chestnut mushrooms	cremini mushrooms
chickpeas	garbanzo beans
clingfilm	plastic wrap
cocoa powder	unsweetened cocoa
cornflour	cornstarch
courgette	zucchini
dark muscovado sugar	dark brown sugar
desiccated coconut	if unavailable, substitute unsweetened shredded coconut
dried chilli flakes	red pepper flakes
fast-action dried yeast	instant yeast
fibre	fiber
filo pastry	phyllo pastry
flaked almonds	slivered almonds
frying pan	skillet
green/orange/red pepper	green/orange/red bell pepper
griddle pan	grill pan
grill (noun); grill (verb)	broiler; broil
groundnut oil	peanut oil
hand-held electric whisk	hand-held electric mixer
haricot beans	navy beans
heavy-based	heavy-bottomed
icing	frosting
icing sugar	confectioners' sugar
kitchen paper	paper towels
light muscovado sugar	light brown sugar
mangetout	snow peas
mixed spice	allspice or apple pie spice
pak choi	bok choy

UK	US
passata	strained tomatoes
plain flour	all-purpose flour
plant-based double cream	plant-based heavy cream
plant-based mince	plant-based ground meat
plant-based natural yogurt	plant-based plain yogurt
plant-based single cream	plant-based light cream
porridge oats	oatmeal
pudding basin	pudding bowl
pudding rice	white short-grain rice
rapeseed oil	canola oil
rocket	arugula
round-bladed knife	blunt knife
self-raising flour	self-rising flour
sieve	strainer
soft light brown sugar	light brown sugar
soya cream/milk	soy cream/milk
spring onions	scallions
sugared almonds	Jordan almonds
tea towel	dish towel
tomato purée	tomato paste
wholemeal	whole wheat

Index

apples 48, 122, 132
apricot & sunflower muffins 42
artichoke hearts 95
asparagus frittata 52

bacon (vegan) 74, 113
bananas
  banana & pecan loaf 116
  banana & sultana drop scones 45
  banana fritters with raspberry sauce 132
  banana, sultana & walnut bread 116
  blueberry & banana French toast 16
  blueberry pancakes with banana 16
  frosted banana bars 121
  mixed berry smoothie 32
  power bars 48
  quinoa porridge with caramelized banana 35
  sesame & banana flapjacks 48
  toffee & banana pancakes 31
beans
  borlotti bean & pepper bruschetta 51
  broad bean & pea crostini 55
  chilli beans with jackfruit 96
  chilli sin carne 96
  chilli tacos 90

  chunky tomato & bean stew 68
  edamame & pea soup with pesto 66
  edamame & pesto soup 67
  home-baked beans on toast 22
  Mediterranean beans 64
  mushroom & black bean omelette 19
  Puy lentil & butter bean salad 87
  quick chilli beans with vegan sausages 23
  quick quesadillas 77
  spicy bean burgers 106
  spicy bean enchiladas 76
  spicy edamame bean & noodle salad 81
  veggie bangers & beans 101
berries 16, 32, 45, 47, 129, 132

caramel sauce 135
cheese (vegan) 19, 52, 55, 57, 61, 64, 67, 73, 74, 76, 77, 90, 94, 95, 103, 105
cherry risotto 136
chicken, plant-based 57, 71, 77
chickpeas
  chickpea & spinach omelette 19
  chickpea salad 52
  chickpea, tomato & pepper salad 58
  chunky chickpea & lentil dahl 93

chunky tomato & bean stew 68
flatbread, roasted veg & hummus 82
lentil, mustard & chickpea soup 73
no-cook lentil chickpea salad 73
spicy chickpea & tofu curry with quinoa 98
spicy chickpea curry 99
chocolate (vegan) 30, 46, 47, 119, 120
chorizo (vegan) 113
courgettes 56, 74
cranberries 122, 129
cupcakes 135, 138, 139
custard, vanilla soya 125, 130

drop scones 45

flapjacks, sesame & banana 48
flatbread, roasted veg & hummus 82

granola 30
grapes 136

jackfruit, chilli beans with 96
jam roly-poly 125

leeks 71
lemons 25, 125, 139
lentils
  chunky chickpea & lentil dahl 93

coconut dahl with toasted naan fingers 93
lentil bolognese 94
lentil, mustard & chickpea soup 73
lentil, tofu & red pepper chilli 91
no-cook lentil chickpea salad 73
Puy lentil & butter bean salad 87
Puy lentil & sun-dried tomato salad 78
Puy lentil stew with garlic bread 79
spicy chickpea curry 99
tikka lentil koftas 80
veggie sausage hotpot 110

mangoes 25, 130
maple granola 30
mince (plant-based) 56, 76, 90, 96, 100, 102, 103
muesli 39
muffins 42, 47, 129
mushrooms 19, 20, 26, 110

noodles 72, 81, 104
nuts 20, 21, 30, 39, 46, 48, 116, 119, 120, 135, 138, 139

oats 21, 25, 30, 32, 39, 48
oranges 42, 122, 123, 125, 138

pad Thai 104
pasta 71, 74, 95, 105, 113
peach & orange muffins 42

peanut butter cookies 131
pears 129
peas 55, 64, 67, 105
peppers 51, 57, 58, 91
pesto 64, 67
pitta breads 57, 61
pizza, cheat's pepper 57
potatoes 29, 103
power bars 48

quesadillas, quick 77
quinoa 35, 98, 126

raita 80
raspberries 35, 125, 132
rice 126, 136
rocky road, high-protein 46

sausages (vegan) 23, 36, 101, 105, 110
spinach 19, 26, 58, 73, 109
spotted dick 124
strawberry oat smoothie 32
sweet potatoes 36
sweetcorn 26

tahini sauce 56
tempeh 81
toffee & banana pancakes 31
tofu
  frittata 52
  high-protein tofu & vegetable noodles 72
  lentil, tofu & red pepper chilli 91
  marinated tofu with vegetables 72

mushroom tofu scramble 26
pad Thai 104
spicy chickpea & tofu curry with quinoa 98
spinach & sweetcorn tofu scramble 26
spinach, tomato & tofu curry 109
tofu with pak choi & spring onions 84
tomatoes 26, 64, 76, 77, 95, 110
  chunky tomato & bean stew 68
  griddled Greek-style sandwiches 61
  potato bread with tomatoes 29
  salads 52, 58, 78, 87
tortillas 68, 76, 77, 90
tuna (vegan) 71

yogurt 25, 47

About the Author

ROSE WYLES is a fully qualified plant-based nutritionist and lifestyle enthusiast, with diplomas in Vegan Nutrition, Raw Nutrition and Child Nutrition for Vegans & Vegetarians. Rose possesses a deep passion for crafting delicious and nutritious plant-based meals, and she has transformed the lives of countless individuals through her expertise in a whole-food, plant-based diet. She has dedicated her career to helping others adopt this lifestyle and reap the many benefits it offers. With her extensive knowledge of nutrition science and culinary skills, Rose has become a trusted source of information and inspiration for those looking to improve their health, lose weight and embrace a more sustainable way of eating.

www.thevegannutritionist.co.uk
X @vegannutrition1
@the_vegan_nutritionist

INTRODUCTION BIBLIOGRAPHY
'Association of Animal and Plant Protein Intake With All-Cause and Cause-Specific Mortality'; PubMed, 2016 (nih.gov)

'Consumption of Nuts and Seeds and Health Outcomes Including Cardiovascular Disease, Diabetes and Metabolic Disease, Cancer, and Mortality: An Umbrella Review'; PMC, 2022 (nih.gov)

'Government Dietary Recommendations'; Public Health England, 2016

'Twin research indicates that a vegan diet improves cardiovascular health'; News Center, Stanford Medicine, 2023 (med.stanford.edu/news)

'Vegan and Omnivorous High Protein Diets Support Comparable Daily Myofibrillar Protein Synthesis Rates and Skeletal Muscle Hypertrophy in Young Adults'; ScienceDirect, 2023 (sciencedirect.com)